TOP 12 NYMPHS FOR TROUT STREAMS

HOW, WHEN, AND WHERE TO FISH THEM ~ 2ND EDITION

SKIP MORRIS

All flies tied by Skip Morris

Photography, illustrations, and cover design by Carol Ann Morris

Copyright © 2022 by Skip Morris

All rights reserved.

No part of this book may be reproduced in any form or by any electronic or mechanical means, including information storage and retrieval systems, without written permission from the author, except for the use of brief quotations in a book review.

ISBN 978-0-9884476-9-1 (paperback)

CONTENTS

1. A Few Great Flies, Dollars Saved 1
2. The Rules of the Game 5
3. Gold Ribbed Hare's Ear 15
   Nymph #1
4. Bead Head Pheasant Tail 20
   Nymph #2
5. Copper John 25
   Nymph #3
6. Bead Head Prince 29
   Nymph #4
7. Pat's Brown Rubber Legs 33
   Nymph #5
8. Glo-Bug, Pink 36
   Nymph #6
9. San Juan Worm, Brown 41
   Nymph #7
10. Burk's Bottom Roller, Hare's Ear Special 46
    Nymph #8
11. Bead Head Fox's Poopah, Olive 50
    Nymph #9
12. March Brown Spider 54
    Nymph #10
13. Bitch Creek 59
    Nymph #11
14. Zebra Midge 63
    Nymph #12
15. A Quick Review 68
16. Bugs, Eggs, and Worms 71
17. Nymph-Fishing Methods 85
18. Just the Essential Stuff, Made Plain 120
    Epilogue 128

About the Author 129

1

A FEW GREAT FLIES, DOLLARS SAVED

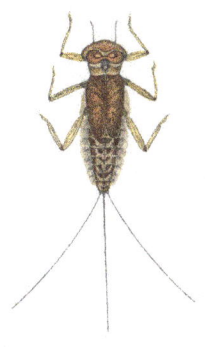

This book (or booklet, small book—whatever it is, I'll just call it a book from here on) is a steal.

Why?

Let me explain.

Most new fly fishers have been through the following ordeal. You stand in a fly shop, blinking in confusion at the many rows of compartments filled with tiny flies and big flies and pale flies and dark flies and brightly colored flies from plain to fancy to outright bizarre and of all shapes and all sizes, or you're sitting there frowning at your computer screen that's displaying page after catalog page—so many pages!—each covered with all sorts of flies, and all you really want to know is: Which ones do I actually *need*?

If that sounds like you, then what you actually need isn't flies at all. What you need is help. You need someone who truly understands trout flies and who will present you a short list of proven, red-hot fly designs that are easy to acquire, and then to explain how, when, and where each of these flies is fished.

At this point, I take a bow.

Because I'll be that someone.

Why me?

Because I *do* understand trout flies (I've written eleven books about fly tying and flies, ink-and-paper books published by real publishers), and I *will* (soon) present you a small number of excellent flies that work in an amazing number of fishing situations. And, yes, as this book's title promises, I'll explain to you how to fish each fly, when to fish it, and where it's best fished.

There are many, many things I can't do: I can't dance, can't snow ski, can't solve difficult math problems, ride a unicycle, speak French, and on and on. But set you up with a modest number of killer trout flies, flies that make an excellent and versatile team, and teach you how to make those flies catch trout? *That* I can definitely do. And will.

But I started out telling you what a bargain this book is, and now that we've examined the strain and tangle that fly selection can easily become for the new fly fisher, and how I can help tame that for you, it's time for me to explain why I believe this book will save you far more than its piddling cover price.

Imagine yourself back in that fly shop or looking through the fly pages of an online catalog. This fly looks good. This one looks like a bug a trout would eat. That one looks like a bee—maybe trout eat bees...

Soon, you've selected, say, two dozen flies. You take them fishing. You find your trout don't want any of them. Why don't they want them? Because your trout are scarfing underwater insects called caddisflies and you have no flies that look like caddisflies. So you buy more flies, ones that look like caddisflies. You return to your trout. Again, your trout don't take your flies. Why? Because no caddisflies are around. Now your trout are taking the rising pupae of a tiny insect called a midge.

So, you buy more flies, midge flies this time. You return to the river, your rod rigged with one of your new midges—but now your trout are concentrating on *stoneflies*.

Help! you think—does it ever *stop*?

Yes, it does stop, right here, with this book.

My point: if you'd started with this book, you'd have bought only a small, versatile, and proven selection of trout flies—before spending a lot of money on flies you don't need and your trout don't want.

Right now, a trout fly costs around two dollars. How many useless flies at that price equal the small price of this little book? Few indeed.

See? This book is a steal because odds are high that it will actually *save* you money. Spend just a few bucks, save a lot more.

The wasted time and the frustration this book will help you avoid, they count too, right?

This is a very practical guide to trout flies and to achieving success with them on trout streams. Imagine you're standing in a stream right now—how do you decide what fly to tie on? You want that *right* fly that will hook trout after trout rather than a plain *wrong* fly that will go ignored cast after cast, but which fly is right? The information you'll learn here will lead you to that right fly, and tell you how to fish it so that it catches you trout. You catching trout: that's really the whole point, isn't it? It is to me. And it is to this book.

There's more. This book will also teach you about the creatures these 12 flies imitate, providing insight that will also help you catch trout (while making fly fishing more interesting and more fun).

2

THE RULES OF THE GAME

What's a Nymph?

There are several primary categories of trout flies—dry flies, emerger-flies, streamers...—but the focus of this book is a specific kind of fly called a "nymph." A nymph-fly imitates, or at least resembles, an underwater insect or similar creature that trout eat. Nymph-flies are a huge part of fly fishing trout streams; in fact fishing nymphs probably accounts for a third of all trout fly fishing. And because trout eat more underwater insect forms than anything else, artificial nymphs should *probably* account for half, even two thirds.

This is a book about nymphs-flies; all 12 of the flies we'll explore in it are nymph designs.

It's About Streams—Fly Fishing Has Always Been (Mainly) About Streams

Yes, trout "streams"; the word's right there in the book's title. So this book focuses not only on nymphs but specifically on nymphs for catching trout in streams. And that's ideal—trout streams (and creeks and rivers, which are really the same thing—flowing waters—differing only in size) are where about 80 percent of all fly fishing is practiced. So, bottom line: we're going to focus on a very natural and deadly type of trout fly (the nymph)—12 outstanding ones, actually—and on the most effective ways to fish them in the waters where most fly fishing goes on (streams).

The Big Deal

"But," you ask, "why do I need help with trout flies—what's the big deal?" Fair question. Answer: well, I've already explained that without guidance, you, as a new fly fisher, can find yourself simply *overwhelmed* by the superabundance of flies out there, and going broke buying too many. Or (as I also explained) you might buy the wrong flies. Or, once on the water—with a sound selection of excellent flies—you might choose the wrong one; in other words, you might fish a good fly but at the wrong time or in the wrong place or in the wrong way and come up trout-empty. And that's why I'm here: I'm going to prepare you by outfitting you with killer flies, and by teaching you how to choose the correct one for conditions—to choose the one that'll catch trout. And teach you *how* to fish it effectively.

"Oh come on," you say, "really, how many different flies can there be?" Well, take books; they're a good example of just how many trout flies lie in wait out there to overwhelm you. I just checked the website of a prominent fly-fishing book distributor, and it currently carries 250 different book titles about flies, which doesn't account for the titles it *doesn't* carry and the ones that have gone out of print. You might want to sit down before I tell you how many fly designs (which fly fishers normally call "patterns") exist, in case you get dizzy. Okay, here goes: even if you consider only *widely popular fly patterns*, there are at least thousands of them—probably *tens* of thousands.

Is that overwhelming enough for you?

Now that I've got you thumping a pencil on a tabletop or popping your knuckles or whatever it is you do when you're anxious, I'll present the good news: You don't need *thousands* of trout flies, much less *tens* of thousands, to go out and catch a trout in a stream. In fact, as nymph patterns go, you can get along very well with only a small number of them that are proven and well-chosen. As I've already said, with 12. Just 12. Honest.

I'll go a step further and state—with the experience of having written several books on fly *fishing* (as opposed to the fly *tying* ones I mentioned earlier) behind me—that with just 12 nymph patterns you can regularly catch even very difficult angler-wise trout, the sort that really test a fly fisher's skills.

So Few?

"Only 12 nymphs," you ask, "but now that you've told me how many flies are out there, how can that possibly be enough?"

In my mind, it all goes back to a rule I love to state, a rule I put into the following words some years ago after seeing it proved time and again:

How you fish a fly is *at least* as important as which fly you fish.

In other words, fish the *perfect* fly improperly or poorly for discriminating trout and you'll catch few, if any of them. But fish a just-adequate fly well and you may clean up with those same fussy trout.

I've noticed that especially among new fly fishers there's a notion, sometimes conscious, sometimes subconscious, that if you carelessly chuck that ideal fly out there—the *best possible* fly for the current conditions—the trout will always come racing for it. It is unrealistic at best, and downright silly to any seasoned trout fly fisher. For example, if you let your ideal fly drag when it should be drifting free (or drift free when it should be moving), that fly will probably fail, unless the trout are in a truly forgiving mood. Take a fly that imitates a mayfly nymph (just ride along with me here. You'll find out what a mayfly nymph is soon enough): it mustn't only *look* like a mayfly nymph, mustn't only match its size and shape; it must *behave* like just another mayfly nymph if it's going to convince trout that it is, in fact, a mayfly nymph. There are sometimes multiple ways to effectively fish a trout fly for specific situations, but usually many more ways to fish it *in*effectively. We'll concentrate, of course, on the best ways for fishing each of our 12 nymphs, fly by fly.

The Two Big Categories

This is a good time to tell you about imitative nymphs and attractor nymphs, since the 12 flies below include both. As they should. *Imitative* nymphs do just what their name suggests: they imitate *real* nymphs. (Or they may imitate nymph-like creatures that may not technically *be* nymphs. Sometimes imitative nymphs imitate things that live underwater that aren't even close to being actual nymphs, such as fish eggs and aquatic worms.)

Attractor nymphs may look almost imitative or may look plain bizarre—the point is that at least *something* about an attractor nymph doesn't add up, something keeps it from truly resembling any real nymphs or nymph-like creatures. That's intentional—attractor nymphs are *supposed* to be weird. They're not supposed to imitate anything.

It's obvious why trout eat imitative nymph patterns: it's because they think they're real, edible creatures. Attractor nymphs aren't so easy to explain. There are theories having to do with trout curiosity, with the need to sample new potential food sources, and more. What really matters is that maybe around one third of the time you'll catch more trout on crazy attractor nymphs than on nymphs that look like real trout feed.

And that's why attractor nymph patterns are among the 12 nymphs to come.

Theories aside, I think the whole phenomenon of attractor-fly effectiveness can be summed up in two words: Go figure... To this I would add: Don't think about it too much; just try fishing attractor nymphs when imitative nymphs fail.

Twelve Yes, But...

By now you've probably guessed that you'll need at least some of the 12 nymph flies in more than one size. Good guess. If the Gold Ribbed Hare's Ear, for example, imitates mayfly nymphs (which it does) and mayfly nymphs run from small to large (which they do), shouldn't your Gold Ribbed Hare's Ears run this same range? Of course they should. And that's why I've provided the most useful sizes for this and the rest of the 12 nymphs. But if you eventually feel the need to go larger or smaller than the "most useful sizes" that I recommend, go ahead.

You'll also need more than one of each fly pattern in each size—what if, let's say, a size 14 Bead Head Pheasant Tail nymph is just slaying trout and no other nymph pattern will do? Do you want to sweat it out every time you feel a trout on the line because this might be the fish that breaks off your *one* killing fly? Of course you don't. And believe me: I've sweated over last flies all too often. So bring at least *two* flies of each *pattern* and each *size*. Three is better.

A Backup Plan

Even though these 12 nymph patterns are commonly found in fly-shop bins and on the pages of online and paper catalogs, you may not be able to easily find every one of the 12. That's because your local fly shop may have replaced one of the patterns with a local favorite. Or the shop, or the online company where you get your flies, may be out of it. So as a backup, I've provided two alternate fly patterns for each of the 12 nymphs—that way you'll almost surely find all the flies you need. The alternates really do fill in effectively for the originals, and all of the alternates, like the originals, are tied by major fly companies so they're out there on the market and therefore normally pretty easy to find.

For the Tier

Of course if you tie flies, you won't need the alternate patterns—you can tie exactly what you want whenever you want, no waiting, no substituting. If you do tie flies, or might someday take up the craft, I've provided the "dressing" or "pattern," that is, the materials and a few tying details, for each of the 12 nymphs.

(Disclosure: you're going to see Daiichi hooks, with only one exception, recommended in the dressings. That's because 1. each hook model is one I trust after too many hours of fishing it to count, 2. I'm on the Daiichi pro staff, and 3. I'm on the Daiichi pro-staff because I believe Daiichi makes excellent hooks. There: full disclosure achieved.)

The Tungsten Factor

A lot of nymphs these days have metal beads for heads—a

bead's weight hurries a nymph down to the trout, before currents sweep it downstream to the end of the line and back up. If you're a tier, you have a choice: tie the nymphs to come, the ones that call for beads, with conventional metal beads or, instead, with tungsten beads. If you buy your flies, you may still get a choice, since one catalog or fly shop may offer a particular nymph pattern with a standard bead while another offers it with a tungsten one. So...

Tungsten is much heavier than the metals used in standard beads, and in many of the quick western rivers I fish most, tungsten-bead nymphs fish best; they cut efficiently down through quick currents to the trout. But in slower or shallower rivers, a nymph with a standard metal bead may be just right. I can tell you for starters that almost all largish to big rivers usually seem best to me with tungsten bead nymphs. But if you have to get nymphs with conventional beads and they're for a big, heavy river, no sweat—just add "split shot," tiny weights that crimp on, up your leader, to hurry the fly's descent.

Selecting From Among the Hordes

A word on how I chose these patterns. First, a fly had to be so thoroughly proven that no sane person could argue against its effectiveness. Second, I had to have proven that fly's effectiveness to my own satisfaction (by fishing it, of course). Third, it had to be a truly popular fly, the kind that regularly shows up in fly shops and catalogs and is therefore easy to put your hands on. (Yes, this last issue really *isn't* an issue for those who tie their own flies, but this is a book for both fly tiers *and* buyers, so...) All the nymphs in here fulfill my three criteria. But there's a fourth—and it's critical.

My fourth criteria is that the 12 flies must function effectively as a *team*; in other words, that they cover so many trout-stream situations that you nearly always have a reasonable fly to show the trout no matter what mood they're in or what form of food they're seeking. (Provided that what they're seeking can be represented at all by an artificial nymph.) Of course, it could happen that you need a dry fly or even a streamer, rather than a nymph, to move the trout. But it's really common for stream trout to want a nymph. A nymph pattern fished in one of the six methods to come will usually move trout as well as or better than any other kind of fly.

So, bottom line: this is a calculated *set* of nymph patterns that work together to keep you catching trout in streams.

The Fishing Methods in Detail

Note that instead of just mentioning in an offhand way the main six methods for fishing these 12 nymphs, I describe each method at some length and provide illustrations to make sure everything is made plain. And the six methods are all together in one convenient place so you can jump to them whenever you need them. (If I had mixed them in with everything else all through the book, you'd spend half your time searching around for them.) When, for example, you read about how to fish a nymph called the Pat's Rubber Legs, you'll see a number and a title—"#1. Standard Indicator Nymph Fishing"—and then you can go to that numbered method at the end of this book and read all about it.

New and Old—But All are Outstanding

Some of these nymphs, such as the Gold Ribbed Hare's Ear and the Bead Head Pheasant Tail, are older flies or updated versions of older flies—but they're *legendary* older flies that reprove themselves year after year, and a few of them have been around long enough to have convinced generation after generation of fly fishers. Others, like the Pat's Rubber Legs and Burk's Bottom Roller, are still fairly

Here We Go...

Well, there it is, then: the plan on which this book is based and the reasons for basing it on that plan. And, now, here are those excellent, deadly 12 trout nymphs trusted by many—some by literally millions—12 nymphs for trout streams that together can do so much more than a mere 12 nymphs logically should be able to do.

By the way, if you've read some of my real ink-and-paper books you know that I've designed a heap of fly patterns and you may also know that many of them are tied commercially and offered in fly shops and in the catalogs. (And if you didn't know, now you do.) I believe in my patterns—*absolutely*. But none of them is as widely available for purchase as the 12 below. Besides, presenting one of my own flies as among "The Top 12 Nymphs" seemed a bit, oh...tacky. I did, however, include two of my own as substitutes (the Ultimate Skip Nymph and the Gabriel's Trumpet, Gold). I invite you to give them a try; they've caught a great many trout for me.

3

GOLD RIBBED HARE'S EAR
NYMPH #1

- **Substitutes:** Bird's Nest, Ultimate Skip Nymph
- **Most useful sizes:** 18, 16, 14, 12

Fly fishers find irresistible any fly they can describe as "buggy," by which they clearly mean "suggestive of a bug." (Never mind that my dictionary instead associates the word with horse-drawn carriages and insect infestations.) Well, *buggy* indeed by the fly-fishers' lexicon is the Gold Ribbed Hare's Ear nymph. It's a nymph that's been around, in its current form, for at least 45 years —I have books in my library that prove it—and catching uncountable trout the whole time.

There's a version of this fly with a metal bead for a head—actually, there's a bead-head version of about every popular nymph these days. You're welcome to take a spin with the bead version— which does catch trout—but I went with the original lightly weighted version (only windings of lead-substitute wire at its core for modest weight) because 1. there will be plenty of bead-head nymphs to come in this book, and 2. lightly weighted nymphs can be fished in ways that beaded nymphs can't, and some of those are good ways.

The scruffy mottled-tan-brown Gold Ribbed Hare's Ear (or GRHE) nymph is a natural for imitating mayfly nymphs of middling shades, and there are quite a few such nymphs in many North American trout streams, from coast to coast. (For information on mayflies—or any of the other insects and creatures these 12 nymph flies imitate—see "Bugs, Eggs, and Worms" at the end of this book.) So if your river or creek contains lots of mayflies—and most do—the trout in that water are used to finding and eating them and the GRHE will always be a promising choice of nymph. For specifically imitating nymphs living on the bottoms of streams, you'll fish it with method #1. (Standard Indicator Nymph Fishing) detailed at the end of this book. In slowish, fairly shallow currents, you may do fine with letting the GRHE sink under its own modest weight. But you'll need either split shot on the tippet or a trailer-nymph rig (all of these are described under method #1.) to get the bead-free GRHE to the trout holding down near the riverbed.

Somewhat pale to medium-shade smaller stonefly nymphs, such as the nymph of the little Yellow Sally, and immature bigger stones, such as the Golden Stonefly—they're all well imitated by the GRHE. Yes, stonefly and mayfly nymphs differ from one

Gold Ribbed Hare's Ear

another, but overall they're much the same in form. And those differences are less apparent in smaller to medium-size nymphs (that is, the range imitated by the GRHE) than in larger ones. Mayfly nymphs and stonefly nymphs hide and cling and creep about the bed of a river (and get swept from it by currents to hungry trout) through much of the normal trout season making the GRHE a consistently sensible choice from spring through fall, and there's no good reason not to try one in winter.

But perhaps you turn a few river stones in the shallows and find an abundance of little stonefly nymphs clinging to them—these nymphs are probably crawling for shore to hatch and the trout are surely gobbling up the ones that make missteps (stoneflies hatch by creeping along the bottom, unlike most mayflies which hatch in the open. But we'll get to all that later). If those little stonefly nymphs come anywhere close to the shading of the GRHE, then it no longer matters that the fly pattern can imitate mayflies and stoneflies both —right now it's imitating *stoneflies* only. To imitate stonefly nymphs with the GRHE you'll fish with Standard Indicator Nymph Fishing, just as you would for imitating mayfly nymphs along a riverbed.

Getting back to mayflies, if they're hatching (the nymphs swimming up and then appearing as winged adult insects on the water) and the trout seem to be rising to take them at the surface but are leaving no bubbles after their rises and showing not their open jaws but possibly their dorsal fins and tails, you probably won't catch many trout on a dry fly or floating "emerger-fly," a fly that imitates a partially hatched insect. Rise-disturbances consistently lacking that telling bubble and nose mean the trout are feeding not *on* the surface of the water but just *under* the surface, almost certainly on the nymphs swimming to the top of the water to squeeze from their obsolete nymph-shucks and unfold their new wings for a few days of life up in the air. So if you find a mayfly hatch and trout feeding at the water's surface but not actually poking their noses out to take down something floating on top, fish your GRHE with method #3. (Dry Fly and Dropper) described at the end of this book. Because the GRHE is fairly lightweight, a dry fly of only modest-size, such as an Elk Hair Caddis or Parachute Adams, will probably hold it suspended and put the GRHE right where the trout are feeding. But remember: the bigger the nymph when fishing Dry Fly and Dropper, the bigger the dry fly you'll need to support it. I would expect to fish *at least* a size 14 Elk Hair Caddis dry fly, well greased with floatant, to support a size 16 GRHE (and I'd prefer the Elk Hair Caddis in size 12).

This is where the standard GRHE's lack of a heavy bead really pays off—it's modest weight holds it down under the surface, but allows a dry fly to suspend it. Perfect! You now see the logic behind including this beadless nymph in the 12.

Czech nymph fishing requires at least one heavy fly, and the GRHE is too light to serve as that. But if the water's neither deep nor swift, one heavy nymph and a standard GRHE may be just right. I like to put the heavy fly on the point and the GRHE up from it as a dropper, but, that's just me. (See method #4. Czech Nymphing).

Fishing methods for the Gold Ribbed Hare's Ear:

- Standard Indicator Nymph Fishing (#1.)
- Dry Fly and Dropper (#3.)
- Czech Nymphing (#4.)

For the fly tier: Gold Ribbed Hare's Ear

HOOK: Heavy wire, standard length to 1X long, sizes 18 to 10. (I prefer the Daiichi 1560.)

THREAD: Brown 8/0 or 6/0.
WEIGHT: Lead-substitute wire.
TAIL: Hare's mask guard hairs. Many tiers like mottled-brown partridge flank or pheasant tail—almost any soft tan or brownish feather fibers make good tails.
RIB: Small oval or narrow flat gold tinsel.
ABDOMEN: Hare's mask dubbing.
WING CASE: A section of mottled turkey primary.
THORAX: Hare's mask dubbing, added rough and heavy, picked out at the sides to suggest legs.

4

BEAD HEAD PHEASANT TAIL
NYMPH #2

- **Fly Designer:** Al Troth
- **Substitutes:** GB (Gold Bead) Black Bird's Nest, GB Flashback Pheasant Tail (a Pheasant Tail nymph with a gold bead and a shiny back)
- **Most useful sizes:** 18, 16, 14

Bead Head Pheasant Tail

First, you should know that there are two nymphs called the Pheasant Tail. There's Englishman Frank Sawyer's, which is sort of an unkempt-looking thing that, indeed, catches trout. But the one we're looking at here is the creation of Montana fly-fishing guide Al Troth, who was a superb fly tier and who created another trout fly as wildly popular as his Pheasant Tail: a dry fly called the Elk Hair Caddis.

Al's Pheasant Tail is an organic sort of design, and a handsome one. Like so many popular nymph patterns, his Pheasant Tail, also known as the Troth's Pheasant Tail, woke one day to find its small head of tight thread-turns replaced by a shining metal bead. You can argue that adding a bead, especially one that's way too large to represent a real insect-head, to this normally convincing pattern makes it *un*convincing, but no one who knows the fly will buy your argument—the Bead Head Pheasant Tail has a great track record that confirms it as an effective nymph. Gleaming-gold and -silver beads wind up on all sorts of old nymph patterns and then the newly crowned versions go out and catch one trout after another.

I think these unnatural bead-headed nymphs catch trout because they still look pretty much like real nymphs, and because, if fished well, they act like them. Hypothesizing aside though, as I said, they work.

They also work, in part, because those metal beads hurry them down to the bed of a stream, and the stream bed is where trout spend most of their time holding and feeding. It's the plainest sort of logic: If the nymph is near the fish, the fish are most likely to take the nymph. The bead takes a Bead Head Pheasant Tail down near the fish.

The Bead Head Pheasant Tail nymph (which from here on I'll refer to by the acronym BHPT), being dark, sort of balances out the Gold Ribbed Hare's Ear—you have a slightly pale nymph (the Gold

Ribbed Hare's Ear or GRHE) for imitating real nymphs of around that same middling to lightish shade, and a dark nymph (the BHPT) for imitating *dark* real nymphs. A team. Of course, they're not quite a matched team since one carries the weight of a metal bead and the other doesn't, but, close enough.

You can always just buy the original Pheasant Tail which lacks a bead, to strike a better balance with the unweighted GRHE. Or you can buy both the bead-head version of the GRHE (there is one, and it's popular and consequently easy to find) *and* the BHPT, so that you end up with a lighter-colored nymph and a dark one both with beads. Personally, though, I think you'll do fine with the original beadless GRHE and the beaded BHPT I'm recommending. With a little adjusting (adding or omitting split shot on the tippet, placing the nymphs in different positions on a trailer-nymph rig, etc.) you can fish them in about the same ways at the same depths. This will all make more sense as you get to know the six nymph-fishing methods at the end of this book.

Okay, on to the specifics of fishing the BHPT nymph. First, Standard Indicator Nymph Fishing (#1. of the methods described at the end of this book). You can simply fish the BHPT below a strike indicator, letting the weight of its bead carry down and hold down this nymph, or you can add split shot on the tippet if needed—whatever gets the fly down in front of a trout nose. If you want to fish a trailer rig (also described under method #1. at the end), go ahead; normally you'd put a larger and very heavy nymph on the main tippet and trail the BHPT, but you can arrange any two flies in a trailer rig any way you like.

In standard indicator nymphing you typically "search," for trout; that is, you fish a plausible nymph wherever a trout might be holding and you assume he's currently open-minded about what he'll eat (which the deep trout that standard indicator fishing reaches often are). However, just before a hatch of mayflies—

ideally, mayflies that are dark in their nymph stage—a BHPT deep below an indicator can clean up: the trout are down there in the safety of depth snapping up the nymphs that are showing themselves in their pre-hatch jitters or rising on their way up to hatch and along comes your BHPT looking like just one more of those swimmy nymphs, and...fish on!

Similar to standard indicator nymphing is the Hopper Dropper method (#2. among the methods at the end of this book), and it's a natural for the BHPT. Hopper Dropper fishing relies on a small heavy nymph, and that's just what the BHPT is.

And then there's Czech Nymphing (#4. among the methods at the end). The BHPT could certainly serve for that. Nymphs for Czech Nymphing are often heavy and of modest to small size. The BHPT is heavy. Of course tied with a *tungsten* bead it's *really* heavy. Combine it in a Czech-nymph rig with one or two lighter nymphs (the GRHE perhaps?) for light currents and mild depth, or with another heavy nymph or two for water deep, quick, or both.

Fishing methods for the Bead Head Pheasant Tail:

- Standard Indicator Nymph Fishing (#1.)
- Hopper Dropper (#2.)
- Czech Nymphing (#4.)

For the fly tier: Bead Head Pheasant Tail (Al Troth)

HOOK: Heavy wire, standard length to 1X long, sizes 18 to 12. (I prefer the Daiichi 1560.)
BEAD: Copper, or black or gold or silver metal bead (for extra weight, use a tungsten bead). For a size 18 hook, 3/32-inch (2.5mm);

for sizes 16 and 14, 7/64-inch (3mm); for a size 12 hook, 1/8-inch (3.5mm).

THREAD: Brown 8/0 or 6/0.

TAIL: Pheasant-tail fibers.

RIB: Small diameter natural-color copper wire.

ABDOMEN: Pheasant-tail fibers.

WING CASE and LEGS: Pheasant-tail fibers. Pull the fibers forward over the thorax for a wing case and bind them at the hook-eye, bind a few of the pointed tips on each side as legs, and then snip off the remaining tips and bind them under the thread head.

THORAX: Peacock herl.

5

COPPER JOHN

NYMPH #3

Top view of the Copper John, showing the bright bar that runs up its epoxy-domed wing case.

- **Fly Designer:** John Barr
- **Substitutes:** Gabriel's Trumpet, Gold; Rainbow Warrior
- **Most useful sizes:** 18, 16, 14

A nymph pattern of somber elegance, the Copper John is primarily an attractor. Sure, it looks something like a mayfly or stonefly nymph, but that gleaming abdomen of copper coils and especially that brilliant bar flashing from its back don't fit the image of any insect. When convincing imitative nymph patterns produce poorly or not at all, I show the trout something strange, something curious—an "attractor" nymph, one that's a little odd or just plain bizarre. The Copper John, having a golden bead and a metallic abdomen and a flashing back, falls into the middle of that range.

There are those who think of this fly as a reliable imitation though—who's to say they're wrong? John Barr himself, who created the Copper John, says in his book *Barr Flies* that he uses the fly in its range of color variations in rivers to suggest the nymphs and larvae of mayflies, stoneflies, caddis, and midges. As reasonable as all that seems, I still can't envision this fly as anything but an attractor nymph—but so what? It's a killer attractor nymph. And I'm probably wrong about the imitative angle and John's probably right.

If you're purchasing your Copper Johns, the standard, original pattern I'm writing about here is now often referred to as the "Copper Copper John," or "Copper John, Copper." There are so many variations of this fly around today that the extra "Copper" in the name seems to clear up any confusion.

Regarding the fishing of the Copper John, I'll start with John's first intended duty for his nymph: the Hopper Dropper method (#2. at the end of this book). The fly's a natural for this work—it's often tied small (so it won't drag down the big supporting dry fly), it's heavy for its size (despite its small hook, its bead and copper-wire abdomen and the lead-substitute wire inside it all make it go down and stay down where the trout are holding), and its abdomen gives off a soft gleam while its wing case flashes brilliantly as the fly twists in the current (flashes that catch the eye of a trout, regardless of fishing method).

Of course the Copper John is a fine fly for suspending below a strike indicator (#1. Standard Indicator Nymph Fishing). And though it's a heavy fly, a split shot or two up the tippet can be the right addition for fast, deep currents. Try it with a trailer-nymph rig (also described in #1.) as the trailer behind a big nymph.

Its serious weight makes the Copper John a fine nymph in a Czech-nymph rig (#4. Czech Nymphing).

The original Copper John wears a bead of standard metal, standard weight. But you can buy it (or of course tie it) with a tungsten bead. Generally, go with the standard bead if your streams aren't deep and aren't swift. Or just go with what you like.

Fishing methods for the Copper John:

- Hopper Dropper (#2.)
- Standard Indicator Nymph Fishing (#1.)
- Czech Nymphing (#4.)

For the fly tier: Copper John (John Barr)

HOOK: Heavy wire, 2X (or 1X) long, sizes 18 to 12. (I prefer the 1X long Daiichi 1560, but the original hook for the Copper John was longer: the Tiemco 5262.)
BEAD: Gold metal. For size 20, 5/64-inch (2mm); for sizes 18 and 16, 7/64-inch (3mm); size 14, 1/8-inch (3.5mm); size 12, 5/32-inch (4mm).

WEIGHT: Lead-substitute wire over the front third or half of the shank only.

THREAD: Black 8/0 or 6/0.

TAIL: Dyed-brown goose biots.

ABDOMEN: Natural-color copper wire.

WING CASE: One strand of pearl Flashabou over a strip of black Thin Skin. Atop the wing case, one drop of epoxy glue. (Note: work with epoxy only with good ventilation, such as outdoors crossways in a breeze. Do not inhale its vapors.)

THORAX: Peacock herl.

LEGS: Mottled-brown hen back (saddle). (I prefer natural-brown partridge.)

6

BEAD HEAD PRINCE
NYMPH #4

- **Fly Designer:** Doug Prince
- **Substitutes:** Bead Head Purple Prince, GB (Gold Bead); Zug Bug
- **Most useful sizes:** 12, 10, 8

If you're reading everything in order here, then you just read my thoughts on the Copper John nymph as an attractor pattern (I say it is) versus as an imitative pattern (some say it's both)—well there's no such debate regarding the Bead Head Prince nymph: until the day real nymphs grow long, white, gently curved *horns*, it's an attractor and *only* an attractor.

On the whole, the Prince is a pretty standard design for an imitative nymph: its biot tails are common on nymph patterns; peacock herl in a nymph body is even more common (just go back and look at the Pheasant Tail and Copper John); a bright rib gussies up the bodies or abdomens of many popular nymphs (example: the Gold Ribbed Hare's Ear); and hackle fibers for legs?—*classic*. The bead? As I said earlier, bead-head nymphs these days are *everywhere*, and at this point the bead has been forgiven its oddness and lots of imitative nymph dressings include one. So, all of that considered, we actually have a plausible imitative nymph.

Until...we get to those insane white *horns*. Truly weird. No aquatic form of insect I've ever seen has had its back topped with two long horns, white or otherwise.

But those horns do seem to make a difference. What does a trout think when it sees them on a Bead Head Prince? Probably something like, *This* I've gotta check out. He moves to it, notices that the rest of the nymph looks insect-like and therefore edible, and, suddenly, you've got a trout on the line. I realize this all sounds a bit shaky, implausible, but the Prince has proven itself over decades as a winning fish-catcher. There's really no debate. And that's why, of course, it's among the 12 nymphs here.

Because the Bead Head Prince (like the original Prince Nymph) is most often tied on a 2X long hook and through hook sizes that run up to plain big, I think of this as a middling to largish pattern, a click or two larger than the average Bead Head Pheasant Tail or

Copper John. I believe most fly fishers see it about this same way. Yes, there are small Prince Nymphs and Bead Head Princes out there. But even so, you've got the Copper John to cover your attractor-nymph needs in size 14 and smaller. Let larger Bead Head Princes cover your middle range.

The Prince started out bead-free as simply the Prince Nymph, but it grew way too popular to avoid getting a bead. Personally, I'm glad it got a shining metal bead planted on it during the bead-fly revolution—the bead only adds more brightness to an already fairly bright fly, and no fly suits brightness better than an attractor pattern.

The first approach to fishing the Bead Head Prince is Standard Indicator Nymph Fishing (method #1. at the end of this book). You can fish the Bead Head Prince all alone or trailing off the bend of another, typically bigger, nymph in a now-common trailer-nymph rig (also described under method #1.); or, of course, buy or tie a big one, a size 8, and make it the big upper nymph in the rig.

The Bead Head Prince is a solid choice for Hopper Dropper fishing (method #2.)—it's about as bright as the Copper John (which was originally *designed* for this setup) and nearly as heavy. Just make sure you tie on a Prince not so large that it'll drag down the big dry fly.

How about Czech Nymphing (method #4.)? This method most often includes smallish nymphs—but certainly not always. Sometimes a big nymph suits Czech Nymphing best, that is, it catches the most trout. So, sure, Czech nymph with your Bead Head Princes.

Fishing methods for the Bead Head Prince:

- Standard Indicator Nymph Fishing (#1.)
- Hopper Dropper (#2.)

- Czech Nymphing (#4.)

For the tier: Bead Head Prince (Doug Prince)

HOOK: Heavy wire, 2X (or 1X) long, sizes 16 to 6. (I prefer the Daiichi 1710.)
BEAD: Gold metal. For a size 8 hook, a 5/32-inch (4mm) bead; for a size 6, 5/32- (4mm) or 3/16-inch (4.6mm).
THREAD: Black 8/0, 6/0, or 3/0.
TAIL: Dyed-brown goose biots.
WEIGHT: Lead-substitute wire. (Taper the ends with a little dubbing.)
RIB: Fine oval gold tinsel (some prefer silver).
BODY: Peacock herl.
HACKLE: Brown hen-back (hen-neck).
WING: Two long, white goose biots, spread into a narrow "V". (Many tiers mount the biots curve-down, but they look more appealing to me when mounted curve-up. Down or up is really a matter of aesthetics, not fish-catching.)

7

PAT'S BROWN RUBBER LEGS
NYMPH #5

- **Fly Designer:** Pat Bennett
- **Substitutes:** Black Rubber Legs; Jimmy Legs, Tan/Brown
- **Most useful sizes:** 8, 6

The Pat's Rubber Legs—and I mean through its whole assortment of color variations—is plainly based on the old Black Rubber Legs pattern. Pat Bennett just juiced up that fine old design, tweaked it into the 21st century. But it's clear that he did the right juicing because you'd be hard-pressed to find a trout-river fly guide in the West these days who doesn't tie Pat's nymphs onto his or her clients' tippets. It's popular in the East too. The fly is an unqualified hit.

Converting the Black Rubber Legs into the Pat's Rubber Legs involved a switch from straight rubber-strand for legs and tails to a flattened slightly snaky rubber-strand called Flexi Floss—the curved strands look more natural than the stick-straight originals to my eye. The addition of antennae (absent in the Black Rubber Legs): nice touch. Sliding forward the legs (they're evenly spaced up the body of the Black Rubber Legs) to put them where they should be, in the thorax, to *really* imitate a stonefly nymph, just made solid sense (although the old Black Rubber Legs certainly proved itself for stonefly duty, regardless of leg-spacing).

And imitating a stonefly nymph is what Pat's Rubber Legs does best, at least in my view. Pat's fly is normally tied big because it is normally used for imitating the *huge* Salmonfly and Golden Stonefly nymphs. These are common names for mottled darkbrown to gold stonefly nymphs and nearly black ones common in trout streams across North America (they're talked about mostly as western but, actually, they're spread from coast to coast).

Stonefly nymphs can live only in moving water; in fact they need pretty lively currents since they depend on those currents to provide oxygen to their inefficient gills. So, normally, medium to fast currents are appropriate places to fish a big-stonefly imitation, such as the Pat's Rubber Legs.

I wouldn't hesitate to fish a Pat's Rubber Legs any time in a trout stream—why would any sane trout refuse such a big, meaty mouthful, especially one that, even after the giant stones have hatched and their big nymphs are gone, looks pleasantly familiar?

The obvious method for fishing this great heavy nymph is Standard Indicator Nymph Fishing (method #1. at the end of this book).

Guides seem to love running a smaller trailer nymph off the bend of a Pat's Rubber Legs (the trailer rig is also described under method #1.), and guides know what to do in order to catch trout otherwise they wouldn't still be guides.

The only other sensible method in my mind for fishing a Pat's Rubber Legs is Czech Nymphing (method #4.). A *big* point fly isn't the norm with the Czech method, but it can be, and Pat's fly is heavy enough to do the job (nymphs for Czech Nymphing are usually quick sinking) so, why not?

Fishing methods for the Pat's Brown Rubber Legs:

- Standard Indicator Nymph Fishing (#1.)
- Czech Nymphing (#4.)

For the fly tier: Pat's Brown Rubber Legs (Pat Bennett)

HOOK: Heavy wire, 3X long (Pat likes a slow-curve shank), sizes 8 and 6 for the big stoneflies, down to size 14 for smaller stones. (I prefer the Tiemco 200. The Daiichi 1260 is my second choice. These are nearly interchangeable hooks in design. But according to my eye, and to my cheapo calipers, the 200 is a shade thicker of wire. So I tend to use the 1260 for big dry flies and the 200 for nymphs when I want to use this French-curve style of hook.)
WEIGHT: Lead-substitute wire.
THREAD: Black (or brown) 6/0 or 3/0.
ANTENNAE (optional): Brown Flexi Floss (rubber-strand).
TAIL: Same strands used to make the antennae.
LEGS: Same strands used to make the antennae.
BODY: Brown chenille.

8

GLO-BUG, PINK

NYMPH #6

- **Fly Designer:** The Bug Shop
- **Substitutes:** Surreal Egg; Mop Fly, Pink (often, the Mop Fly is offered only in size 10, and size 10 is fine)
- **Most useful sizes:** 14, 12

Even though I definitely consider the Glo-Bug a trout fly, you need to know that if you go to buy the pattern from a catalog or a fly shop you'll probably find it among what they label as "Steelhead" or "Alaska" patterns. Most fly fishers use Glo-Bugs for pretty exotic fishing—migratory steelhead, Alaska rainbow, and Dolly Varden for example—and most of it a far cry from a brown trout living out its life among mayfly hatches in a mountain stream, the sort of fishing most fly fishers consider, well, standard.

Steelhead and Alaska...it's true that Glo-Bugs get a lot of use in those categories. I guess that's why it continually surprises me that the fly can be deadly on everyday lower-48 trout. I mean, an average steelhead lugs around perhaps ten times the body-mass of an average mountain brownie, and spends most of his life in the ocean among jellyfish and kelp while dodging seals—a lifestyle that would shock our sedate little backwoods brown. And Alaska? I've done that—that's *crazy* fishing. Imagine 20-pound salmon swarming in brackish lagoons, rainbow trout over 10 pounds gobbling up gobs of flesh torn by river currents from the carcasses of dead, spawned-out salmon (and at times, gobbling the eggs of those salmon), and Dolly Varden char racing for every lose salmon egg tumbling downstream. It's really like that, at the right place and the right time...with luck.

You get the point: the situations most fly fishers consider appropriate for an egg-fly such as the Glo-Bug are nothing like the average fly fisher's neat little trout stream. Nevertheless—a Glo-Bug may *slay* the trout in that stream.

I told you all that so you'd understand why Glo-Bugs don't normally show up among the trout flies, and so you'll understand why you may get confused when you go to buy Glo-Bugs, and may even be told, "Those aren't for day-to-day *trout* fishing." But if you're told something like that, ignore it, because I've caught scads of day-to-day trout on Glo-Bugs. And I've seen trout, mountain brown trout included, go just *mad* for Glo-Bugs—darting nervously, rushing to them, chasing them down. These fuzzy egg-flies don't nearly always clean up on trout—sometimes they're pretty useless for them—but when they do work they can work well, or way beyond well. Fishing Glo-Bugs can get wild, and that's big fun. And that's why the Glo-Bug's here in this fly collection: once in a while it moves or even inspires trout when all other flies seem to make them yawn.

The logical time to fish the Glo-Bug is when something—the rainbow trout or whitefish or migratory salmon or such—is spawning in the river. And that is in fact a fine time to show the trout a fish-egg fly. But the truth is, Glo-Bugs can work when nothing's spawning, and in sizes far too large to even nearly match any fish egg the trout have ever seen.

Man can they work.

There are lots of Glo-Bug colors and other fly fishers tell me they all work (even chartreuse, black, yellow, green—weird, eh?). I trust pink most of all the colors, but I've had great success with orange and with red Glo-Bugs. Still trying to find my place with black, chartreuse...

A fish egg drifts freely with the current in a stream, of course, and so must a Glo-Bug that imitates an egg. So Standard Indicator Nymph Fishing (method #1. at the end of this book) makes perfect sense with this fly. I've sometimes used a Glo-Bug successfully as a trailer behind a big, heavy nymph (also described under #1.).

Hopper Dropper fishing (method #2. at the end of this book) with a Glo-Bug as the nymph? The only snag lies in getting the unweighted Glo-Bug quickly down and fishing. A tiny split shot halfway up the trailer tippet above a knot is an option (though split on the dropper tippet of a Hopper Dropper rig does complicate casting, that tiny cannonball weight swinging around...), but if you tie your flies, a metal bead on the hook's shank at the front of the Glo-Bug's fuzzy body will do the job.

I've never heard of anyone using a Glo-Bug as a dropper in a rig for Czech Nymphing (#4. at the end), and haven't tried it myself, but considering how effective the fly can be, it makes perfect sense to me to try it that way.

Regarding that optional bead in a Glo-Bug, I use beaded Glo-Bugs more often than the standard unweighted ones. I just slip a metal bead (black, or pre-painted pink, red...) onto the hook and up to its eye, tie and trim the fly, done. The bead's mostly hidden in the fluff of all that egg-yarn. Unweighted Glo-Bugs are actually pretty buoyant; but a few firm squeezes underwater will eventually soak them enough to let them to sink.

(Note: the latest stand-in for the Glo-Bug is the Mop Fly. Both patterns are fuzzy and many come in fish-egg colors. Go with the Mop if you like. I've not fished it enough to judge it. Sure have caught scads of trout on Glo-Bugs though...)

Fishing methods for the Glo-Bug, Pink:

- Standard Indicator Nymph Fishing (#1.)
- Hopper Dropper (#2.)
- Czech Nymphing (#4.)

For the fly tier: Glo-Bug, Pink (The Bug Shop)

HOOK: Heavy wire, curved shank (a standard egg-fly hook, although I also like a humped scud-pupa hook), sizes 16 to 4. (I prefer the Daiichi 1120.)
BEAD (optional): A metal bead, regular or tungsten, pink, or any color.
THREAD: Pink 6/0 or 3/0.
BODY: Pink egg yarn, with one small bunch of doubled red or orange egg yarn to create a spot. Basically, you bind one or two sections of yarn atop the shank, one or two below the shank (all the

thread windings as one tight, narrow collar), add the red or orange yarn for the spot by doubling it over the thread and pulling it down into the rest of the yarn (top or bottom), draw it all back and whip finish and then trim the thread. To trim the yarn, pull it all up *firmly* and give it a quick snip. Some tiers pull the bottom yarn down and snip, then the top yarn up and snip.

9

SAN JUAN WORM, BROWN
NYMPH #7

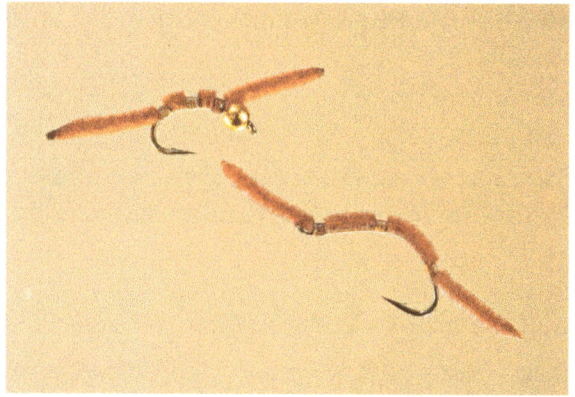

- **Substitutes:** Bead Head San Juan Worm, Squirmy Wormie
- **Most useful sizes:** 14, 12

Ready for another oddity among nymph patterns, fully as odd as the Glo-Bug—yet, still, another proven trout-taker? Here it is: the San Juan Worm. The name comes from the famously, and notoriously, difficult San Juan River of New Mexico where the pattern was developed. The San Juan holds some really persnickety, overfed, angler-savvy trout. I know this, I've fished there.

The San Juan Worm is a very simple fly, but it's a clever fly nonetheless. Apparently, before it was born, no one had previously seen the connection between Vernille (also called "Ultra Chenille") and aquatic worms: specifically, that they look about the same. Even the colors of both the tying material and these underwater versions of the common earthworm overlap considerably. A natural combination.

But the fly is sometimes tied in a bright orange that I've never seen in an aquatic worm, sometimes in purple, and these are clearly attractor colors. Actually, though, I believe the Worm in any color, even the brown (or flesh-pink or red—yes red) of a real aquatic worm often works just because the trout see it and figure it's edible and then eat it without any awareness at that moment that aquatic worms exist.

But I also believe that trout take the Worm, at least in natural colors, because 1. aquatic worms are substantial gobs of delicious protein (delicious to trout), 2. some streams hold lots of them, and 3. trout learn to watch for them and jump them when they appear.

Aquatic worms, what kind of worms are those? you ask. Well, I'm no entomologist (if entomology covers worms...which I doubt. Anyway, I'm no worm aficionado either) but I *can* tell you that there are worms in trout streams that look pretty much like the earthworms living in my lawn. I recall finding them under rocks in the streams of my youth and staring in confusion—how did these earthworms get *here*?

My friend Dave Hughes is, if not a bona fide entomologist with an official paper document to prove it, a longtime dedicated amateur one, and knows a lot about most every living thing that trout eat in a stream. In his book *Pocketguide to Western Hatches* he says, "Aquatic worms are most common in the silt and sand of spring creek and tailwater substrates" and that they "do not swim" and consequently are "always taken on or near the bottom" by the trout. Now you know a bit about aquatic worms. If you want to know more, just jump ahead to the section "Bugs, Eggs, and Worms."

So, "always taken on or near the bottom," says Dave? That's a natural scenario for Standard Indicator Nymph Fishing (method #1. at the end of this book) provided you tie on a Worm with a bead built into it or add split shot up the tippet. And of course, the trailer-nymph rig (also described in #1.) is a fine fit with the San Juan Worm as the trailer.

As the dropper in a Hopper Dropper rig (method #2. at the end)? You bet. Especially if you're fishing one of the newer variations of the San Juan Worm with a metal bead built into it. Without the bead you can still make this work, but don't expect the Worm to get down to the trout very quickly (though you can always add a tiny split shot to your dropper tippet and see how that complicates your casting). I recall a fly-shop salesman in Montana describing to me how he fished Worms on Hopper Dropper rigs to land a couple of dozen cutthroats, browns, and rainbows during a day's drift fishing on a local river. Strong evidence for the Worm fished by this approach.

Czech Nymphing (method #4.)? Sure—an unweighted San Juan Worm or a Worm with a bead makes perfect sense in the rig and fished by this method. Although an unweighted Worm will need a heavy fly or two in the rig to drag it down.

Dry and Dropper (method #3.)? Not really… I mean, the Worm fly seems a bit large for that work to me; I like a small nymph below a modest-size dry fly for Dry and Dropper fishing, and the Worm's typically pretty big tied on any hook. Besides, the Dry and Dropper is really a rig for almost-rising trout during insect hatches. And Dry and Dropper involves a short dropper tippet, yet the Worm is supposed to be fished deep, remember?

Still, the original unweighted Worm is unusually lightweight with no metal rib or core of wire or anything else other than the hook to draw it down, so it might not drag a modest-size dry fly under. And the Worm, especially in unlikely colors, probably does serve as an attractor at times, and an attractor can be fished at any depth. Hmm...maybe the San Juan Worm's not such a poor choice for Dry and Dropper after all... Honestly, I haven't tried it this way, but perhaps I, and you, should.

Regarding the Worm with a metal bead versus the unweighted original, I feel they're both useful. But I suggest you start out with the unweighted version, simply because it's the most versatile, and then add the beaded version later if you choose.

Fishing methods for the San Juan Worm, Brown:

- Standard Indicator Nymph Fishing (#1.)
- Hopper Dropper (#2.)
- Czech Nymphing (#4.)
- Dry and Dropper (#3.) maybe...

For the fly tier: San Juan Worm, Brown

HOOK: Heavy wire, humped shank (scud-pupa hook) sizes 14 to 8. (I prefer the Daiichi 1120.)
BEAD (optional, not included in the original pattern): Black, copper, or gold bead (an ultra-heavy tungsten bead is an option).
THREAD: Brown 8/0, 6/0, or 3/0.
BODY: Brown Vernille or Ultra Chenille, bound by three thread-bands up the hook's shank, melted at both ends.

NOTES: If you include a bead, the front end of the Worm will angle up, but not too steeply if you don't run the thread up tight against the bead. The front end of the Worm tipping up...what's the big deal?—this is supposed to be a wriggling, twisting worm with all sorts of bends in it, right?

10

BURK'S BOTTOM ROLLER, HARE'S EAR SPECIAL

NYMPH #8

- **Fly Designer:** Andy Burk
- **Substitutes:** Tungsten Surveyor, Jigged Tungsten Hare's Ear
- **Most useful sizes:** 12, 10

The most significant feature of the Burk's Bottom Roller: it's *really* heavy. The second most significant: there's little built into it to slow its descent in a trout stream—no hackle, no tail, no gills. Due to its abundant weight and uncluttered form, this is a nymph that goes down, *fast*.

Sometimes you need that. Which is old news to me. I was living in Oregon when I got serious about fishing nymphs, way back in the early 1980s. I selected as my nymph-fishing laboratory the Metolius River. The Metolius is a generally swift spring creek—and no part of it, especially its lower reaches, is anything like what a sane fly fisher would call an actual *creek*. It's a smallish, maybe medium-size river upstream, a plain big one in its lower parts. But it rises from underground springs, and that makes it officially a "spring creek" by the fly-fisher's lexicon. Sometimes, no, *often* fly fishers speak in ways that really don't add up. Yet, somehow, we generally understand each other. It's weird.

Anyway, back to the Metolius. Yes, it's mostly quick, but it's also frequently deep. It's a river of new country formed by volcanic eruptions merely thousands of years old, which might as well be last week to the geologist. It's bed narrows, rushes, and deepens in the tight spots between lava walls, bangs off hard corners of lava, drops off deep in odd places. It's perplexing, fascinating water. It's also a difficult stream in which to get a nymph down to trout.

But I kept at it. I was determined to attain the position of "good nymph fisher," and figured success on the Metolius would be my inauguration. No split shot or bare weight of any kind was allowed on that fly-only stream. So I began tying big nymphs that were little more than lead windings covered thinly with dubbing. I used them to carry down smaller, more-natural nymphs rigged along with them.

In a nutshell: it was a sound strategy, I got my nymphs down to the trout, I caught trout.

We didn't have metal tying beads back then, and were really a long way from having them in tungsten. But I certainly would have had a big tungsten bead for a head on my dubbing-covered lead had that option been available to me. (I'd have used nontoxic lead-*substitute* wire, too, to protect the river and me both, but that wasn't yet out either.) By adding a big bead to my dubbed monstrosity I'd have made it a little like Burke's Bottom Roller.

So now, you have a sense of what this fly is about: it's about cutting down swiftly through deep, heavy currents.

But it's more than disguised weight. It catches trout.

As it should. It looks considerably like a caddis larva and it's plump and looks alive and therefore edible. (It also resembles a less common inhabitant of trout streams, the cranefly larva, which, like the caddis larva, appears as pretty much a sausage.) What's there for a trout not to like?

Fishing methods for the Burk's Bottom Roller? I think of two methods first, and rank them about equally: Standard Indicator Nymph Fishing (method #1. at the end of this book) and Czech Nymphing (method #4.). For indicator fishing I might run a smaller trailer nymph off the hook (covered in #1.).

A heavy fly like this is a natural for indicator fishing, as an alternative to split shot on the tippet.

Not nearly all Czech nymphing involves unusually large or heavy nymphs, but when it does require them, for water quick or deep or both, a Bottom Roller is a fine choice.

I feel this fly is just too heavy for Hopper Dropper fishing (#2. at the end)...but who knows? Maybe a really small Burk's Bottom Roller hung from a particularly large dry fly... Or maybe not.

Fishing methods for the Burk's Bottom Roller, Hare's Ear Special:

- Czech Nymphing (#4.)
- Standard Indicator Nymph Fishing (#1.)

- Hopper Dropper (#2.)...maybe

For the fly tier: Burk's Bottom Roller, Hare's Ear Special (Andy Burk)

HOOK: Heavy wire, humped shank (scud-pupa hook), sizes 14 to 8. (I prefer the Daiichi 1120.)
BEAD: Gold tungsten. For a size 14 hook, 1/8-inch (3.5mm) bead; for sizes 12 and 10, 5/32-inch (4mm); for size 8, 3/16-inch (4.6mm).
WEIGHT: Lead-substitute wire.
THREAD: Beige or tan 8/0, 6/0, or 3/0.
BACK: Strip of mother-of-pearl Sili Skin (or another pearl or clear sheeting such as Stretch Flex or Scud Back). The back goes all the way to the hook's eye, in front of the bead.
RIB: 5X tippet. Run the rib up the back and body and across the top of the bead (over the Sili Skin on top of the bead, that is). I sometimes use copper wire, really any color, and fairly stout (for example: Ultra Wire in size Brassie or, for the largest hooks, medium.)
BODY: Peacock Arizona Synthetic Dubbing in both Light and Dark Hare's Ear, blended (or another rough, shiny dubbing in hare's mask coloring).

11

BEAD HEAD FOX'S POOPAH, OLIVE
NYMPH #9

- **Fly Designer:** Tim Fox
- **Substitutes:** Silvey's Beaded Pupa, Tan; Nitro Caddis, Tan
- **Most useful sizes:** 16, 14, 12

Bead Head Fox's Poopah, Olive

Here's a fine imitation of a caddis pupa, and wherever you fish for trout, across North America and, for that matter, Europe, you'll often need such an imitation. When caddisflies hatch, they hatch as a group, the moth-like adults popping out of the water to flutter about. During caddis hatches, the trout do take the adults and, of course, dry-fly imitations of them. But, probably because new caddis adults are typically quick to fly off the water and beyond their reach, trout tend to concentrate on gobbling up the swimming pupae (and that's no assumption, that's personal experience). This means you'll normally do best during a caddis hatch by fishing an imitation of the pupa. And there are none better than the Bead Head Fox's Poopah.

But be warned: caddis adults on the water aren't always a sign of a caddis hatch. Mature female caddisflies head back to the water to release their fertilized eggs, and when that's afoot, it's dry-fly time—because then, there are no pupae around. (Some female caddis actually swim down underwater for egg-laying, and that's about "wet flies," winged sinking flies, and not related to the subject of this book.)

The Poopah (for short) really carries the look of a living caddis pupa. Its stout abdomen, speckled legs, dark and lively thorax, and even its two antennae all fill out the impression. Its metal bead for a head provides some of the glow that's often discussed with regards to caddis pupae. But the bead serves a more important purpose: it gets the fly below the moving surface of the river and holds it there. That's where the real pupae are mostly taken by trout, below the surface, and that's where your fly will best imitate them and most interest the trout.

To my mind, as the result of my own experience with the fly and with caddis hatches in general, the Poopah is usually best fished on The Swing (method #5. at the end of this book). A caddis-pupa fly on The Swing can be a killer during a caddis hatch. The trout are slamming the quick-moving insects as they're swimming to the surface to hatch; your fly, matching the real pupae, sways and jiggles as though swimming against the current; consequently...*wham.*

If the current from which the caddis are hatching is slow, and my heavy, beaded Poopah is dropping deeper than I'd like it to on The Swing, I'll retrieve it a little, in short strips of line, which also adds to the fly's impression of swimming. But my fly-fishing-author friend Dave Hughes instead employs a technique called the Crosfield Draw, which, in a nutshell, amounts to throwing mends of the line not upstream, as usual, but *downstream*, to swing the fly sideways to the flow and speed up its progress and hold it up off the bottom, or just to keep it swinging at all. Even a light current's tug on a broad arc of fly line really picks up a fly's pace. If you want to read more about the Crosfield Draw and other techniques for fishing flies on The Swing, particularly soft-hackled flies (I'll introduce you to one of those soon) and what fly fishers call flymphs and wet flies, check out Dave's book, *Wet Flies: 2nd Edition: Fishing Soft-Hackles, Flymphs, Winged Wets, and All-Fur Wets.*

Of course, if caddis are coming off in water too slow moving for a proper swing of the bead-headed Poopah, you can always try a March Brown Spider soft-hackled fly—it's unweighted, can imitate caddis pupae, and is the next fly coming up.

Sometimes, trout seek the pupae deeper. When you see caddis popping off all around on the water but few rises or boils—little in terms of trout activity at or just below the river's surface—the trout are likely grabbing the insects down somewhere near the stream bed, early in the pupae's upward swim. Then, you fish your Poopah dead drift in Standard Indicator Nymph Fishing style (method #1. at the end of this book). You can dangle the Poopah as a trailer off a bigger, heavier nymph if you need the help in getting the Poopah down, or add weight to your tippet (both also covered in #1.).

The Bead Head Fox's Poopah—precisely because it has a bead for a head—makes a fine trailer nymph for Hopper Dropper Fishing (#2. at the end).

As a dropper fly in a Czech Nymph rig (#4. at the end)?—you bet. The fly is heavy but not to the extreme, modest in size, just makes sense.

Fishing methods for the Bead Head Fox's Poopah, Olive:

- The Swing (#5.)
- Standard Indicator Nymph Fishing (#1.)
- Hopper Dropper (#2.)
- Czech Nymphing (#4.)

For the fly tier: Bead Head Fox's Poopah, Olive (Tim Fox)

HOOK: Heavy wire, 1X long, sizes 16 to 12. (I prefer the Daiichi 1560.)
BEAD: Gold metal. For size 16, 7/64-inch (3mm); size 14, 1/8-inch (3.5mm); size 12, 5/32-inch (4mm).
THREAD: Black 8/0 or 6/0.
RIB: Small-diameter gold (or copper) wire.
UNDER-BODY: Medium flat pearl tinsel, wound up the shank.
ABDOMEN: Olive standard-diameter Vernille or Ultra Chenille, melted on the rear end. Tight turns of the rib wire secure the abdomen along the top of the tinsel-covered shank.
LEGS: Mottled-brown hen back or partridge fibers.
ANTENNAE: Two pale-yellow wood-duck (or mallard-dyed-wood-duck) fibers.
THORAX: Black ostrich herl.

12

MARCH BROWN SPIDER

NYMPH #10

- **Substitutes:** Partridge and Herl, Starling and Herl
- **Most useful sizes:** 16, 14, 12

Soft-hackled flies go *way* back. But they also keep coming back —that is, fly fishers rediscover them every few decades— because they're plain deadly. And sometimes they're deadly when no other flies seem to work at all. I learned this in a slow and frustrating way. Many times I stood in a stream, throwing dry flies one after another—small and smaller ones, big ones, proven imitations of mayflies and caddisflies and midges, wild attractor patterns—out among trout working the surface of the water. Trout were rising, and that was that. Floating flies seemed the only sensible response.

The problem was: trout were, in fact, *not* rising. Yes, they were showing their dorsal fins and stirring up patches of current—making *imitation* rises—and those imitations were convincing. But I eventually learned that a true rise shows specifically a trout's *nose* above the water—exposed tail tips and dorsal fins prove nothing—and, usually, rising trout leave bubbles. In taking a floating insect from the air, a trout takes in air with it. When the trout goes down, it expels that air and *voilá*: air bubbles.

The reason I saw no noses, no bubbles, is that the trout were feeding just short of the surface. They were feeding so close to the surface, on pupa or nymphs rising to hatch, that their movements stirred the water there creating impressions of rises. This is a fairly common thing for trout in streams to do.

For the fly fisher who doesn't understand or recognize what's going on, this business can be maddening.

Once you do understand it though, the absence of noses, of bubbles, becomes a useful—make that an *important*—tell.

So, at some point, I grew frustrated enough with a bunch of what I assumed were rising trout that I tried a soft hackle. (This was probably around three-and-a-half decades ago. Yes, I'm an old guy.) I had a few in my fly boxes and I'd read about how to swing them. And: I caught a whole bunch of trout on them that day, trout that had just ignored a lot of dry flies and floating emerger-flies.

To say this event made an impression on me would be to grossly understate the effect.

From then on, I tried to watch carefully for the signs that would tell me if trout were really rising or just creating false indications of rises—that is, I watched for noses and bubbles. When there were none, I tied on a soft-hackled fly. Sort of changed my life.

On the advice of my fellow fly-author and friend Dave Hughes, I tied and kept on hand a lot of March Brown Spiders. The March Brown Spider is the soft-hackle analog of the Gold Ribbed Hare's Ear nymph: rough, a little bristly, a little sparkly, a patchwork of neutral shades. It's a combination that loosely suggests a lot of pupae and nymphs. Suggests them effectively too; I proved that to my satisfaction long ago. Though there are lots of other good soft-hackled flies around, you're not going to find a soft-hackle more reliable and versatile than this one.

Like the Bead Head Fox's Poopah, the March Brown Spider is normally fished on The Swing (method #5. at the end of this book). But there's a big difference between the Bead Head Poopah and the Spider: a metal bead—specifically, the Poopah having one and the Spider having none. This makes the Spider the much lighter of the two flies. Despite that, I don't do a lot to compensate for the weight difference. I just fish the Spider and other true *unweighted* soft-hackles on the swing and expect the fly to ride higher in the water than something with a bead. (I also tie the pattern with a small, conventional metal bead, to keep it submerged in quick currents. You can now buy soft-hackles with beads, but the beadless original version should be your starting choice.) But there's another reason for going with beadless March Brown Spiders.

Davy Wotton, a Welsh expat who guides on the White River and other rich tail-water streams in Arkansas, is a wet-fly and soft-hackle specialist and authority. He feels that a soft-hackled fly is best fished upstream (The Upstream Soft-Hackle, method #6. at the end). Davy knows his stuff, so I've been fishing soft-hackles his way over the past couple of seasons and his way really works. It's not as difficult to manage as you might expect, nor is detecting a strike as tricky as you'd think.

Some longtime fly fishers might question the appropriateness of including a soft-hackled fly among a collection of nymphs, and I can understand why—no old hand at this business is about to label a soft-hackle a nymph. The soft-hackle doesn't really look like a nymph nor is it normally fished deep below a strike indicator or in a Czech-nymph rig as are most nymphs. Of course soft-hackles, other than the rare off-label applications, aren't dry flies, either—they're definitely supposed to stay submerged, if only a little ways down. And if you classify soft-hackles as emerger-flies you have a new problem: nearly all emerger-flies are fished dead drift, *floating*, and *not* on the swing. Really, soft-hackled flies fit only into their own unique category.

So now we know what soft-hackled flies are not, but the question remains, How *does* a soft-hackled fly wind up with a bunch of nymphs? The simple answer: because it's more like a nymph than any of the other major kinds of trout fly. A nymph is fished submerged, typically to imitate an insect, and so is the soft-hackle. *And*, some *true* nymphs are fished on the swing just as soft-hackles are (again, the Bead Head Fox's Poopah...).

Maybe it's not such a stretch after all, including a soft-hackled fly in a book about nymphs?

All that aside, I probably put the March Brown Spider soft-hackle here because it just felt right to do so. Or maybe just because I wanted to. Or maybe because I knew you'd be glad I did when the need for it arose in your fishing.

Fishing methods for the March Brown Spider:

- The Swing (#5.)
- The Upstream Soft-Hackle (#6.)

For the fly tier: March Brown Spider

HOOK: Heavy wire, standard length to 1X long, sizes 18 to 10. (I prefer the Daiichi 1550 or 1560.)
THREAD: Orange (or tan or brown) 8/0 or 6/0.
RIB: Fine oval or flat narrow gold tinsel.
BODY: Hare's mask.
HACKLE: One longish natural-brown partridge-flank or hen-back (hen-saddle) hackle.

13

BITCH CREEK

NYMPH #11

- **Substitutes:** Montana Stone, Rubber Legs Brown Stone
- **Most useful sizes:** 8, 6

There's lots to say about the Bitch Creek—and soon, I'll say it—but first you need to know that it's a nymph that's proved itself to generations of fly fishers, which is exactly why it continues to show up in the catalogs and fly-shop bins. And why it's right here.

Really, that should dispose of any doubts about the effectiveness of the Bitch Creek. From here on, I'll assume it does.

Of course when, where, and how to fish a Bitch Creek is another matter. This nymph pattern has never quite settled in my mind as either an imitation or an attractor. At a glance, it's an obvious match for the nymph of the great Salmonfly stonefly. But at second glance, a red flag pops up: those white antennae and tails just don't make sense—the tails and antennae of the Salmonfly nymph are as near-black as the insect's back and legs.

That said, the orange belly, the black back, the size of the fly (big)—it's definitely one for the Salmonfly hatch. And it's been proven as such, a solid imitation of the Salmonfly nymph.

But the Bitch Creek has caught me lots of trout in streams where all the real Salmonfly nymphs even close to the size of the one I had on were all hatched and long gone, so I've come to trust it as an at*tractor*. Add to that how it's performed for me in streams where no Salmonfly nymphs ever *existed*—what better proof of its worth as an attractor can you want?

The Bitch Creek has a lot going for it: the flashes of its orange underside as it tumbles in the current (suggestive of the pale underside of a Salmonfly nymph, or of any nymph since most are lighter underneath than on top), the soft hackle-legs waving, the rubber antennae and tails swaying... It's easy to imagine trout falling just for the overall insect-like and living appearance of the thing. And maybe their interest starts when they move to it to get a better look at those oddly white antennae and tails.

So, if I need to imitate the hulking nymph of the Salmonfly prior to or early in the hatch, or if I just feel a big, interesting nymph pattern might move the trout, then onto my tippet goes the old reliable Bitch Creek.

The most common and most logical way to fish the Bitch Creek is Standard Indicator Nymph Fishing (method #1. at the end of this book). Hanging such a large and weighted nymph below a standard dry fly is hopeless, and even below a big buoyant dry fly it's...well...pushing the limits, *at best*, so the Dry Fly and Dropper is out and Hopper Dropper fishing offers little promise.

For a trailer rig (also described under method #1.), the Bitch Creek is a good choice for the big upper nymph, the one that gets the smaller one down to the trout.

As a fly for Czech Nymph Fishing (method #4. at the end of this booklet)? Sure.

As a real diver, the Bitch Creek rates a solid seven out of ten. But even a heavily weighted Bitch Creek won't sink as rapidly as a Burk's Bottom Roller will under the weight of its oversize bead and belly full of metal. The hackle fibers in particular slow the descent of the Bitch Creek. I mean, it does get down with purpose, but if you really need a fly that goes down in a *rush*, even while dragging other, lighter nymph flies behind it, the Bottom Roller's a wiser choice.

But you can get any fly quickly deep into swift currents if you crimp enough split shot above it. And split has long been the trusted solution for getting even the heaviest nymphs down when they won't make it on their own.

Fishing methods for the Bitch Creek:

- Standard indicator Nymph Fishing (#1.)
- Czech Nymphing (#4.)

For the fly tier: Bitch Creek

HOOK: Heavy wire, 3X or 4X long, sizes 10 to 2. (I prefer the Daiichi 1720.)

THREAD: Black 3/0, 6/0, or 8/0.
WEIGHT: Lead-substitute wire.
TAILS and ANTENNAE: White rubber-strand (but use black or brown if you like. Makes sense).
ABDOMEN: Orange and black chenille, woven, black on top and orange for the belly.
HACKLE: Brown, one, spiraled over the thorax.
THORAX: Black chenille.

14

ZEBRA MIDGE
NYMPH #12

- **Substitutes:** Beaded Brassie, Copper; Mercury Black Beauty
- **Most useful sizes:** 20, 18

I couldn't in good conscience make up a list of must-have nymphs without including an imitation of that frequently important and more frequently maddening insect: the midge. You can ignore midge hatches and midge-loving trout, in order to preserve your sanity, but you'll pay for your stubbornness if you do.

Midges really can draw trout, sometimes lots of trout, up to sip sedately and steadily at the calm face of a stream. And midges accomplish this despite that they're ridiculously tiny—we're talking hooks of size 18 down to 24, even 26, to properly match the insect. I've seen smaller midges—and I've seen substantial trout up working them. I have a box of *size 32* hooks in my tying room right now. Sharpen a pencil and the exposed lead tip will be significantly longer than an entire hook of this size. I honestly do plan to tie up some midge imitations on them and show them to trout. Why? Because midges—and I mean midges I've seen trout eat—actually get that small. (And because I want to have the right to say I caught trout on size 32 hooks. Sounds just so *impressive*.)

When midge pupae are struggling to break through that ceiling that is water's surface, where air pressure makes the water dense, they spend some time there. Trout know this and often focus their feeding on the abundant pupae collected along or just below the underside of that plane. And there's the real point—midges tend to hatch in great flurries, such heavy numbers that despite their dinky size they, altogether, add up to substantial meat for trout.

And there's another important point in all that: trout often work the helpless pupae rather than take their chances with fully hatched and winged adults that can fly off at any moment. Which means you're wise to approach a midge hatch by starting with the Zebra Midge, a solid midge-pupa imitation.

When midges are hatching, it's all pretty close to invisible, at least to the casual human eye. You've about got to get your nose wet to recognize the tiny mosquito-like adults standing or fussing on the surface of the water before you can assume there are worm-like pupae wriggling just beneath that surface. But your first clue will be trout swirling easily at the top of slow water in steady rhythms to take in one tiny squirming pupa after another. Those trout will likely be feeding not at the surface but just under it. (See "March Brown Spider" earlier for more on just-subsurface-feeding trout.)

During a midge hatch it's hard to beat fishing the Zebra Midge as a dropper off the bend of a dry fly of modest to small size (the Dry Fly and Dropper method, #3. at the end of this book), and that carries the advantage of offering you a winged dry fly easy to spot on the water, as a sort of strike indicator. Let the dry fly pass freely, dead drift, through the rises, until it goes down or jumps, and when it does—set the hook.

I've also done well during midge hatches by letting a lightly weighted midge-pupa fly, the Zebra Midge in this case, drift slowly across the current among rises (The Swing, method #5.). A quick swing of a midge-pupa fly would make no sense and probably catch few trout. Real midge pupae do a lot of just hanging right under the water's surface and some light squirming. But darting off sideways? Nope. However, in the gentle currents midges love, where silt settles as their habitat, a swing of a pupa-fly will be subtle indeed, and close to the movement the trout expect to see.

Trout take midge pupae deeper too. Early in a midge hatch they'll take them deep, before many of the pupae have risen far from the stream bed. And, in fact, trout will take a deep midge pupa about any time. I've found that deep trout that refuse middling to large nymph-flies often have difficulty seeing through the deception of tiny nymphs, enough difficulty that they go ahead and eat them. So when I'm faced with smart, sullen trout holding to the stream bed, I often wind up catching a few (or more) of them with a midge-pupa fly fished down close to their level.

Getting that Zebra Midge down to deep trout is about Standard Indicator Nymph Fishing (method #1. at the end). You can add some weight on the tippet above the fly or use a trailer-nymph rig (also described under method #1.) with the Zebra as the trailer. Both approaches work; I've proven that to my own satisfaction.

Czech Nymphing (method #4.) with a Zebra Midge? Sure. As I've said, careful trout often make errors with tiny flies they wouldn't make with larger ones, providing you a possible advantage you wouldn't get with larger nymphs in a Czech rig.

I've never tried so small a nymph as the Zebra Midge for Hopper Dropper fishing (method #2.) simply because 1. Hopper Dropper fishing is normally about a *small heavy* nymph for a dropper, not a tiny one with only a tiny bead for weight; 2. I wouldn't expect such a tiny fly, even with its tiny bead for assistance, to get down sufficiently below the big dry fly on its own; and 3. as I mentioned earlier, split shot on the dropper tippet of a Hopper Dropper rig is something like a snarl in waiting. So, sure, try a Zebra Hopper Dropper style if you like; just because I haven't tried it doesn't mean it's not effective.

The Zebra likes to vary its name, and now comes in various colors, which can make a chore out of determining if you've found the fly you're looking for. This sort of thing happens a lot with flies that, like the Zebra, have no known originator—there's no one to give the final word on anything. Some catalogs call the Zebra Midge the *Beaded* Zebra Midge. And some call it the Beaded *Silver/Black* Zebra Midge. But my research suggests that the name for the standard pattern, with a metal bead for a head, a black body, and a silver rib is simply, as I've stated it, the Zebra Midge. If you're still confused, just scan the dressing that follows, the photo above, or the photo on the cover of this book.

Fishing methods for the Zebra Midge:

- Dry and Dropper (#3.)

- The Swing (#5.)
- Standard Indicator Nymph Fishing (#1.)
- Czech Nymphing (#4.)
- Hopper Dropper (#2.) *maybe...*

For the fly tier: Zebra Midge

HOOK: Heavy wire, humped shank (scud/pupa hook), sizes 22 to 18. (I prefer the Daiichi 1120.)
BEAD: Silver metal. For size 22, a 1/16-inch (1.5mm) bead; for size 20 and 18, 5/64-inch (2mm).
THREAD: Black 8/0.
RIB: Fine silver wire.
BODY: The black working thread.

15
A QUICK REVIEW

We just covered a great deal of information. Do you remember it all? If I were you, having read through it once, I wouldn't. So below is a very brief reminder of what each fly, essentially, is. Should be enough to spark your memory, to bring up the bulk of the other details.

You're going to get the most out of this little book, though, by reading through it more than once, and probably by reading quite a few times the sections that pertain specifically to your fishing. Anyway...

Gold Ribbed Hare's Ear
Unweighted, for imitating light- to middling-hued mayfly and stonefly nymphs. A good fly for general prospecting for trout.

Bead Head Pheasant Tail
Weighted, imitates darker mayfly and stonefly nymphs. Like the Gold Ribbed Hare's Ear, a good prospecting fly.

Copper John
Especially heavy, imitates nothing (though some would disagree on that point), an attractor fly.

Bead Head Prince
Weighted, an attractor that's on the large side.

Pat's Brown Rubber Legs
Weighted, an imitation of big stonefly nymphs.

Glo-Bug, Pink
Unweighted (though you can tie it weighted), imitates fish eggs but can work wonders where there are no such eggs.

San Juan Worm, Brown
Unweighted (usually), imitates an aquatic worm.

Burk's Bottom Roller, Hare's Ear Special
Very heavy, a general imitation that really goes down and drags a trailer nymph (if one is attached) down with it.

Bead Head Fox's Poopah, Olive
Weighted, an imitation of a caddisfly pupa, a fly to be fished during a caddis hatch.

March Brown Spider
Unweighted normally, it imitates mayflies and caddis about to reach the surface of the water.

Bitch Creek
Weighted, imitates big stonefly nymphs but can be a fished as an attractor and as a pattern for prospecting when prospecting with smaller flies is slow.

Zebra Midge
Lightly weighted, always small to tiny, imitates midge pupae.

16

BUGS, EGGS, AND WORMS

Let's begin here with a reminder you'd be wise to bear in mind as we explore all these creatures that artificial nymphs imitate: lots of flies, nymphs included, imitate nothing. In fact, they're *designed* to imitate nothing. So, non-imitative "attractor" nymphs (examples: Bead Head Prince, Copper John) have no connection with the bugs and other edible and living things that follow.

But lots of nymph patterns (examples: Gold Ribbed Hare's Ear; Bead Head Fox's Poopah, Olive) *do* imitate real trout foods. Here, then, are the things trout eat that the imitative nymphs among the 12 in this booklet do imitate.

Mayflies

A mayfly nymph.

Freshly hatched adult mayflies (called duns)—their bodies arched, the elongated soft triangles of their wings high and slightly parted and tipped gracefully back—are pure elegance. What matters here, though, is that mayflies spend only a few hours to a few days as winged adults but live the bulk of their lives underwater as nymphs. Nymphs trout love to eat.

The nymph of the mayfly is tapered through its slender to slightly stout abdomen. Its thorax (chest, basically) is thicker, with a hump, called a "wing case," containing its future wings, on its back. It has six slender to genuinely stout legs (depending on the variety of mayfly), all extending from its thorax. It usually has two tails, but some mayfly nymphs have three. Its antennae are so tiny as to be unnoticeable to the human eye.

Here, we need to consider the *other* nymph you'll commonly

find in trout streams: the stonefly nymph. It's quite similar to a mayfly nymph but has stouter tails, a thick abdomen not tapered but of constant diameter, not *one* wing case (like a mayfly nymph's) but what appear to be *three* up the back of its thorax, six always-stout legs, prominent antennae, and not the mayfly's dainty head but one that's wide and flattened. A stonefly nymph and mayfly nymph of similar size and coloring, side by side, would be easy to identify for a seasoned fly-fishing bug enthusiast, but a mild challenge for a newbie fly fisher.

So, back to mayfly nymphs, which can run from as tiny as a size 22 hook to as big as a size 4—a stunning range—though most mayflies match hooks of size 18 to 12. The coloring of various mayfly nymphs can be almost black to almost creamy pale—though most mayfly nymphs run brownish to olive in middling to dark shades.

Some sorts of mayfly nymphs live in fairly quick, rocky flows; some live among the weeds of lazy currents; and yet others live in the silt that collects in near-dead water. Mayflies of all kinds can be spread all through a trout stream.

At hatching time, a few up to mobs of the nymphs of one particular mayfly type (Blue-Winged Olive, Western March Brown, Sulphur...—there are many) begin swimming up to free their compacted wings at the surface of the water and fly off (providing trout don't take them first). If you know a particular mayfly will likely begin hatching soon, fish an imitation of its nymph deep until the hatch really gets going and trout are up picking off the duns and the emerging half-duns. Sometimes, even when the duns are everywhere, the trout will stay on the nymphs, catching them usually just under the surface. Then a soft-hackle on the Swing or the Upstream Soft-Hackled Fly approach, or a nymph fished Dry and Dropper style, can kill.

Most mayfly types hatch in this open-water fashion described above. A few swim ashore and climb up out of the water to hatch.

Then the fishing is entirely about soft-hackled flies or Dry and Dropper nymphs (or maybe Standard Indicator Nymph Fishing or Czech Nymphing). That is, until the female "spinners," fully matured adults, start dropping onto the water to release their fertilized eggs; then the low-floating spinners may hold the trout's attention and only a floating imitation—that is, a dry fly not a nymph —will do.

Nymph-flies that can imitate mayflies:

Gold Ribbed Hare's Ear, Bead Head Pheasant Tail, March Brown Spider, Copper John (maybe...)

Caddisflies

A caddisfly larva.

A caddisfly pupa.

The mayfly and stonefly live out most of their lives along the bed of a trout stream as nymphs. The caddisfly lives out most of its life as a "larva," which runs from almost slim to grub-chubby, and is pretty much a cylinder from end to end, though some taper at the ends. The larva has six fairly short legs. A sort of slightly-to-really-stubby worm with small legs clustered up front.

Depending on the particular variety, a caddis larva may hide under rocks, spin a net to live in, or crawl around in the open while dragging around a protective case it's built of pebbles, bark, sand, whatever, containing its abdomen.

Before hatching, the larva matures into a "pupa," the same chunky bratwurst as before, if not chunkier, but now with wing pads along its sides and six no-longer-stubby but *long* legs and long, new antennae. At hatching time, only a scattering up to *hordes* of identical caddis pupae all stroke swiftly for the surface of the water at around the same time. Some caddis varieties struggle at the surface to shed their obsolete shucks and free their new wings, some take less time at this, and some just pop out and fly right off.

Adult caddisflies look a lot like moths that, at rest, fold their wings together over their backs in a wedge that's often described as "tent-like."

Caddisfly larvae and pupae range in size about as widely as mayflies, matching fly hooks of size 22 to size 6, though sizes 16 to 12 are most common. They vary in color too. Some sort of green or olive is common, but others are tan, cream, orange...—there are many caddis colors.

Since caddisflies spend most of their lives as larvae down on or in the stream bed, and some streams hold a lot of them, a nymph resembling a caddis larva can always be a reasonable choice.

During a hatch, imitations of the pupa, usually fished on The Swing, sometimes fished deep and dead drift (Standard Indicator Nymph Fishing and Czech Nymphing), typically out-fish dry flies by a considerable margin. When the female adult caddis return to the water to release their eggs, nymphs are useless; the dry fly is the answer. But the females of some important caddisfly types swim down to deposit their eggs; then a soft-hackled fly fished on The Swing or by the Upstream Soft-Hackled Fly method is a wise choice.

Nymph-flies that can imitate caddis larvae and pupae:

- **Larva:** Burk's Bottom Roller, Hare's Ear Special
- **Pupa:** Bead Head Fox's Poopah, Olive; March Brown Spider

Stoneflies

A stonefly nymph.

Like the mayfly, the stonefly lives out most of its life as a nymph. Then, when the time's right, it creeps to shore and *crawls* out of the water to split and escape its shuck and fly off. I already described the differences in appearance between stonefly and mayfly nymphs under "Mayflies" above, so look there if you're unsure how to tell one from the other. (Recap, stonefly nymph: six stout legs, three wing cases, two tails, two prominent antennae, body fairly consistent in diameter throughout, wide and flat head.)

This skulking way a stonefly hatches couldn't be more different from the open-water squirming or swimming to the surface of a stream that is most mayfly and caddis and midge hatches, an invitation for the trout to feed their hearts out. A stonefly hatch is fairly covert. But all those stonefly nymphs (some of them gargantuan) trying to work towards shore without getting swept off by the swift currents in which they live, and sometimes getting swept off anyway, creates a fine opportunity for trout.

As long as plenty of nymphs are still crawling about the riverbed, from the earliest stages of a stonefly hatch up until the winged adults start appearing in real numbers, an imitation of a stonefly nymph can work wonders on the right day. Standard Indicator Nymph Fishing and Czech Nymphing suit this situation just fine.

The winged adult stonefly is, of course, proof that a stream carries stoneflies (though nearly all trout streams do). The adult stonefly is sort of a stout cylinder from end to end with the same stout legs and prominent tails and antennae as the nymph. The adult stone, however, lays its wings *flat* over its back—that's a good identifying feature, because neither mayflies nor caddis hold their wings back, down, and flat.

The stonefly nymph can live only in quick currents—The Powers That Be cursed it with some pretty lousy gills, so river currents must do most of the work for these second-rate organs. Wherever a trout stream bounces or races along, raise a few rocks and check their undersides. Eventually, you'll probably find stonefly nymphs clinging there.

There are massive stoneflies in streams all across North America. (Though you hear most about the *western* Salmonfly and, to a lesser degree, the *western* Golden Stonefly. Not sure why the eastern ones get so little attention.) But smaller stonefly nymphs can certainly command stream-trouts' attention.

(A special note on nymph-flies and stonefly nymphs here. The Pat's Rubber Legs was designed to imitate *big* stones, and to a lesser degree, so was the Bitch Creek. But small stonefly nymphs and small mayfly nymphs are similar enough that such nymph patterns as the Gold Ribbed Hare's Ear and Bead Head Pheasant Tail, designed for imitating mayflies, do a solid job of imitating both insects.)

Nymph-flies that can imitate stonefly nymphs:

Pat's Brown Rubber Legs, Bitch Creek, Gold Ribbed Hare's Ear, Bead Head Pheasant Tail, Copper John (maybe...)

Midges

A midge pupa.

Midges are tiny. So you might ask, Why would trout bother with them? Answer: Because there are so bloody *many* of them. Midges don't always come off in mobs, but they do often enough that trout half expect them to. So it's wise to go to trout streams with midge imitations tucked away in your fly boxes. Of course I've provided you with only one such imitation here, the Zebra Midge, but one good midge-fly will serve you honorably through a whole lot of midge hatches. And the Zebra Midge is definitely a good one.

A midge spends most of its life as a tiny worm-like, almost-featureless larva, (just as a caddisfly spends most of its life as a tiny to big larva), in the slow, silty parts of a stream. Nearing hatch time, the larva transforms into a pupa (which is similar to the larva but with gills and a swollen thorax; still, no legs out in view yet). At hatch time the pupa wriggles its way inefficiently to the surface of the water (an entirely unimpressive performance in comparison to the caddis pupa's upward dash). The trout are fine with the midge's poor swimming skills; they make it easy prey.

The pupa finally bangs up against the water's skin until it breaks through. Then it splits its shuck and emerges up into air; frees and dries its new wings; rests, standing on its new legs; and finally flies off to mature and, then, to mate.

Midges hatch the year round, and can be important pretty much any time on a trout stream. However the cold months of fall through winter and into early spring are when I find trout most often focused on midges. So regarding your one, fine midge-larva/pupa fly, the Zebra Midge, my point is that you may need it to cover a midge hatch at any time of year.

And, because tiny flies are difficult for trout to identify as impostors, it always carries the potential for fooling trout that have become cautious and cagey, even when no midges hatch.

(Here's an odd/interesting twist: though midges live in both the slow currents of streams and the standing water of lakes—so either nearly dead water or truly dead water—lake midges can match a size 8 hook, yet you'll never see one matching a hook larger than size 18 in a stream. At least I never have after decades of fishing midge hatches all over the western US and western Canada. According to a bona fide entomologist friend of mine, the river midge and lake midge really are *exactly* the same insect. Go figure... Maybe that's why fly fishers call this bug a midge when it's in rivers and a chironomid when it lives in lakes—an attempt to put some conceptual space between the two, for clarity. It does seem to help.)

Nymph-flies that can imitate midge larvae and pupae:

Zebra Midge

Aquatic Worms

An aquatic worm.

Most of what you need to know about aquatic worms is covered in the section on the San Juan Worm. In summary: yes, there are worms that live *in* trout streams (that's right: under the water); yes, they look pretty much like the earthworms in your garden; yes, aquatic worms run pretty much the normal earthworm colors of tan to reddish to the tannish pink of flesh to a true red. Crazy, eh? Garden worms hiding under stones in trout streams and getting on just fine there.

Aquatic worms like to burrow not far into the silt and sand of slower currents in streams. Some live among the shaggy water plants that in some streams blanket the stones. These worms never hatch, of course, as mayflies and caddis and stoneflies do—I mean, if they did, what in God's name would they hatch *into*?

Living in a stream and having no swimming abilities carries risks, especially during periods when the stream is running high and hard, when an aquatic worm can get swept away to the waiting mouth of a trout. Of course an aquatic worm can get caught in the current any old time, and these meaty, wriggly denizens of the muck make fine trout snacks.

Nymph-flies that can imitate aquatic worms:

San Juan Worm, Brown

Eggs

A fish egg.

Most of the fishes in trout streams (trout, of course, and whitefish, sculpins, salmon, dace...) spawn eggs. (Though some may give live birth. Not sure.) And depositing eggs in moving water is an inefficient business at best, probably plain sloppy on average. It's likely, therefore, that often as not, some fish or another is letting loose into a stream those little balls of protein trout love to gobble.

But real eggs in the stream is only one scenario that suggests tying on an egg-fly—trout will often jump such a fly when there seems to be not a single fish egg in the water. It's probably instinctive, since a fish egg is as easy as prey gets and a fine source of fuel, and trout have been eating fish eggs for as long as they've been spawning them. It's easy to imagine Nature wiring the egg-attack response into a trout brain.

Whatever the reason—instinct, curiosity...—egg-flies can work wonders when they theoretically shouldn't work at all. So if nothing appears to be spawning in the stream yet your logical nymph patterns fail, try a Glo-Bug. It may not work or it may work well, or it may work *spectacularly*. If, however, spawning salmon show in your stream, or rainbow trout (or any fish) are fanning gravel for spawning beds, *definitely* give a Glo-Bug a chance.

Nymph-flies that can imitate fish eggs:

Glo-Bug, Pink

17

NYMPH-FISHING METHODS

Notes on Knots

Even though this is really a book about flies, I decided to briefly address knots first. Why? Because all fly fishing is about knots: they hold fly to tippet and tippet to leader and more. They hold together the whole process of fishing a fly. So, as logically follows, they hold together the process of fishing a nymph. Here, then, are the knots I use in my nymph fishing and recommend.

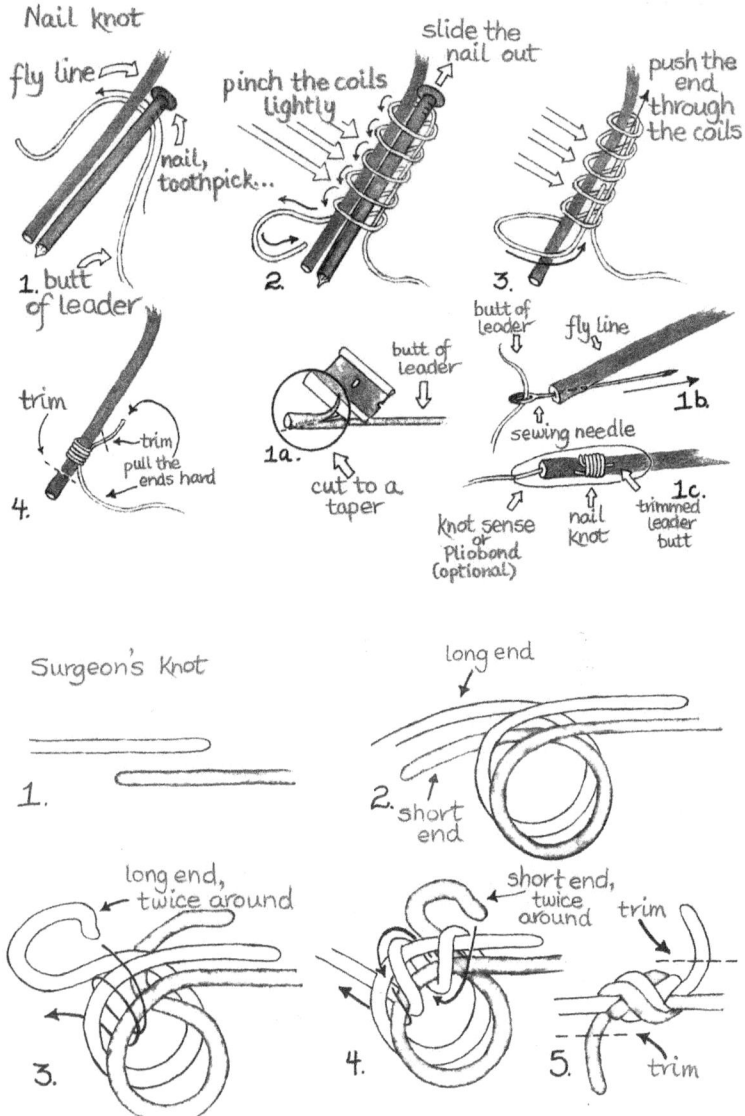

Nymph-Fishing Methods

Improved Clinch & Skip's Clinch

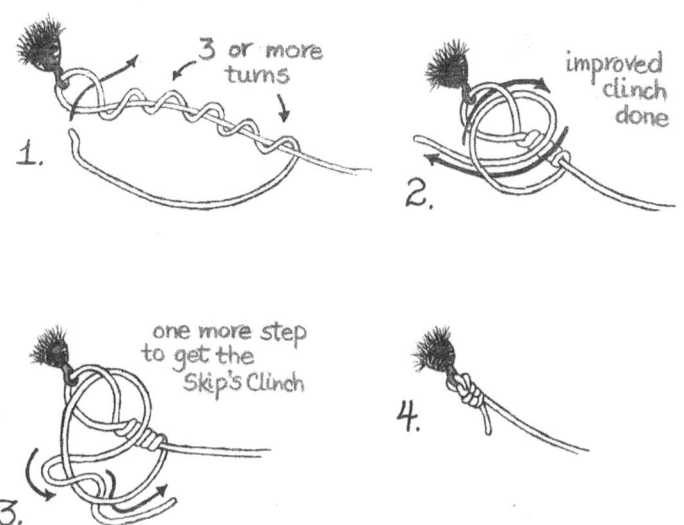

All the above illustrations originally appeared (in color) in 365 FLY-FISHING TIPS FOR TROUT, BASS, AND PANFISH. Reprinted by permission from Stackpole Books.

The nail knot typically attaches leader to fly line (unless the fly line comes with a looped end that can be interconnected with the loop pre-tied at the butt of a tapered leader), and the surgeon's knot (some use a blood knot) attaches tippet to leader. The improved clinch has long been a widely trusted knot for attaching fly to tippet (though I prefer my Skip's clinch, which is simply an improved clinch whose end ran one additional time through the last loop of tippet. Once you know the improved clinch, you'll understand.) That's all standard procedure for trout fly fishing, regardless of fly type. But there are a couple of specific angles regarding knots for nymph fishing in trout streams.

Overhand Knot

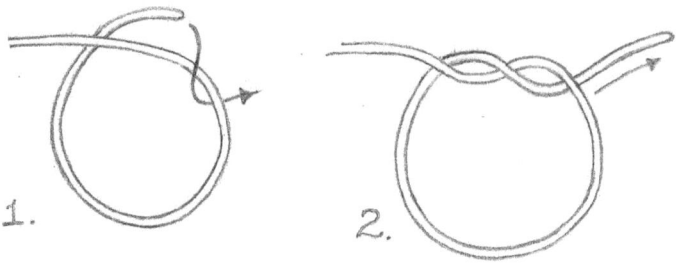

1.

2.

Double Overhand Knot

1. Tie an overhand knot, but do not tighten it.

2. Run the end of the tippet back through the loop a second time.

Split shot, or other weight, is often added to a nymph rig 10 or 12 inches up the tippet to drag the fly down quickly—and a split shot or two can sometimes work wonders in nymphing, getting the nymph down that critical extra few inches, suddenly changing slow fishing to fast. But the long tippets that help nymphs sink create a problem: how do you keep that weight from slipping down the slick, slender tippet to lie against the fly? With nothing to stop it, a split shot or other weight squeezed around the tippet will almost certainly slip at some point. So, you tie a stopper knot in the tippet where you want to add the weight; then you clamp on the split just above the knot.

I did some research on which knot to use for the stopper and found several recommended—there's clearly no standard knot for this business. But most chose a plain overhand knot, the simplest of all knots (it's the one I've always used for this purpose). Some tied three of them close together, some ran the tippet back through the knot's loop twice. But most just tied and tightened an overhand and left it at that.

So, I conducted an experiment: I tied an overhand knot in the end of a foot of 4X tippet, clamped a nontoxic split shot, "BB" size, close above the knot, held one end of the tippet and pulled hard on the shot. The overhand knot did its job well: I had to pull fairly hard before the knot started traveling and the split pushed it off the end of the tippet. I tried it all again with another knot and split shot, same result. So I tied another overhand knot—but *this* time, I ran the tippet through the knot-loop twice. I clamped a split on tightly again and pulled—this time I had to yank really hard before the knot started moving. Another two times through tying this new knot and crimping another split and more hard yanking to move the knot. At this point I ended the experiment—my fingers were sore and I was tired of ruining and throwing away split shot. The moral: twice through the overhand-knot loop is sound insurance for a split-shot stopper.

Morris Loop Knot

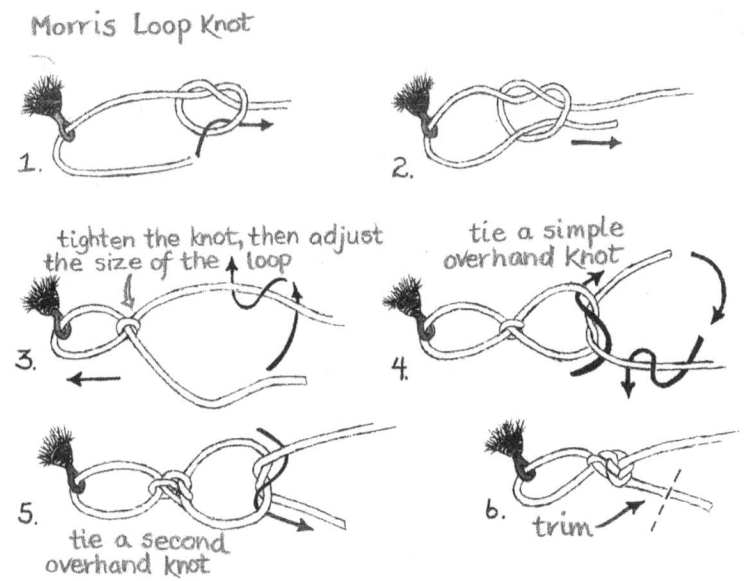

This illustration originally appeared (in color) in 365 FLY-FISHING TIPS FOR TROUT, BASS, AND PANFISH. Reprinted by permission from Stackpole Books.

Another knot I recommend for nymph fishing is a loop knot. There are a few loop knots around: the mono loop knot, the Duncan loop knot, the Rapala... But in my book *365 Fly-Fishing Tips for Trout, Bass, and Panfish* I present the only loop knot I now use, and that's the one I'll teach you here: the Morris Loop Knot. (I call it that to keep my name out there which in turn provides me and Carol food to eat—name recognition tends to boost the scrawny income of a fly-fishing writer, and we like food.) It's actually my favorite loop knot because I can so easily adjust the size of the loop. (Turns out it's similar to one of the several versions of the Homer Rhode loop knot that was around before I came up with my knot.)

If you use a knot that *locks* your fly to your tippet, such as the improved clinch, your nymph can sway around *only* by bending that tippet. Bending, say, 3X tippet (a bit heavy, but a good size for large trout), is a challenge for a size 14 nymph, an average-size nymph for a trout stream. But a knot that allows that nymph to swing around freely on a loop? Just imagine the lively and convincing dance that nymph will perform down there among the trout...

THE METHODS

Here are the six methods for fishing nymphs, the methods I've so often referred to throughout our exploration of all our top 12 nymphs.

Method #1. Standard Indicator Nymph Fishing (and the trailer-nymph rig)

There's always some new way to fish a nymph. In recent years, Czech Nymphing and the Hopper Dropper rig, for example, have caused plenty of chatter and made many converts. As they should have—these methods work. The artificial nymph has left no doubt as to its effectiveness on river trout, so I suppose no one should be the least bit surprised that we fly fishers continue to dream up new ways to make it pay off, ways suited to particular situations or just to reaching trout we couldn't previously pester.

But despite the steady, slow parade of new nymph-fishing approaches, the reliable old strike-indicator style remains the most versatile and (probably) most popular trout-stream nymph-fishing method of all. (As best I can tell, it came out first in Gary Borger's book *Nymphing*, published in 1979. Though Dave Whitlock had worked out a lot of the details, and a similar method, earlier in the 70s.) You can fish a nymph below an indicator close in front of you or way out into a broad river, in currents fast or slow, in water shin deep to neck deep, in pools and riffles and runs and in pockets behind boulders, and all the while catch trout—now *that's* versatile. Indicator fishing remains my baseline approach for trout-stream nymph fishing, the one I think of first and use most often.

Standard Indicator Nymph Fishing starts with the rig. I, and many others use the one that follows. A nymph (weighted, normally) is tied onto a fairly long tippet, usually three to four feet—a long tippet allows a nymph to sink faster than does a shorter one because tippet is the finest filament in the rig and therefore the easiest for the nymph to draw down. A longer tippet, being fine, means less of the heavier tapered leader, which results in a faster descent of the nymph.

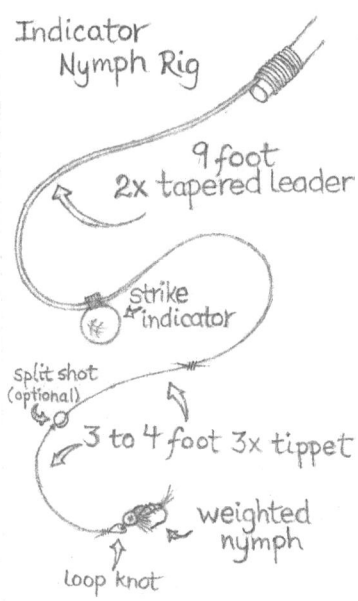

I'll typically tie that tippet to a 9-foot, 2X tapered leader. My tippet is standard or fluorocarbon 3X. Fluorocarbon: sinks better and is (though some question it) more transparent than standard tippet...but *way* more expensive. Standard tippet works fine too; I caught trout on it for decades before fluorocarbon came out. For nymph fishing in smaller rivers and in streams I'll go with a 7 ½-foot 3X tapered leader and 4X tippet, still three to four feet long (though shorter, down to two feet, if the water is truly creek size). I'm always willing to go to ever finer leaders and, especially, finer tippets if the water is very clear, the currents are slow, the trout are annoyingly smart, or any combination of these factors.

A strike indicator comes next. (Despite trying various forms of indicator along the way—yarn, putty, etc.—I've kept returning to the "Corkie," a painted cork ball with a hole through its center that slides up the tippet and is then fixed on the leader with half a round toothpick jammed between the leader and hole. But I'm really liking the Air-Lock indicator ever more, with its screw-on nut that fixes it on the leader, a nut you'd just better not drop or lose—no plastic nut makes the indicator useless.) On average, I'll fix the indicator up from the nymph one-and-a-half times the depth of the water they'll pass through. If the current's really swift, that could be two times the depth; if it's slow, it could be only the actual depth.

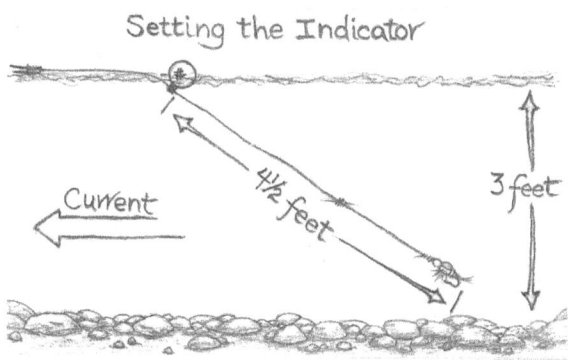

Setting the Indicator

I always use a full-floating line for Standard Indicator Nymph Fishing.

If my nymph isn't going down deep enough or quickly enough, I'll add weight (I use nontoxic split shot) a foot to a foot and a half up the tippet from the nymph (just above an overhand stopper knot, as described above in "Notes on Knots" above). But weight on a nymph tippet is always optional and, in water slow to moderate in speed, shallow, or both, may create more problems than solutions.

Okay, that's how *I* rig for this style of nymph fishing. There are lots of other ways, and many have merit. Still, my way's a good way and it's been good to me over the past, oh, three decades or so. (Though in fairness, my way's pretty much the standard way.)

So, to execute Standard Indicator Nymph Fishing...

1. Stand (or if the water's shallow, slow, or both, and clear, then crouch too) in the stream or on the bank next to promising water.

2. Make a long, smooth casting stroke, with a wide line loop, to throw the rig well *up*stream but not very far out into the flow. Typically, indicator-nymphing casts are short, 15 to 30 feet. (But tricky though it is, chucking the indicator out 40, even 50 feet or farther can occasionally get you trout others don't reach.)

3. Let the strike indicator drift in the current freely, with no drag, as your nymph sinks. (You can always avoid drag on the indicator by "mending," raising the rod-tip and flipping it upstream or downstream to throw a curve in the line.)

As the indicator drifts ever closer, slowly raise the rod's tip to take up much of the slack line. When the indicator is directly in front of you the rod should angle well up (but not raised so high you can't set the hook).

4. As the indicator drifts on past you downstream, slowly lower the rod's tip to feed out line to let the drift continue.

5. When the indicator comes to the end of the line and is dragging straight downstream, cast upstream again—but now you want the indicator to go another foot or two farther out. Keep following this pattern of working the nymph a little farther out each second or third drift. This, and moving your position, will pass your nymph through all the promising water in a systematic fashion.

A trout can grab that nymph any time it's in the water, so watch the indicator for *any* sign that a trout's taken your nymph: a sudden dive underwater, of course, but even a quiver or a stall in drift—these are all reasons to *immediately* tug on the fly.

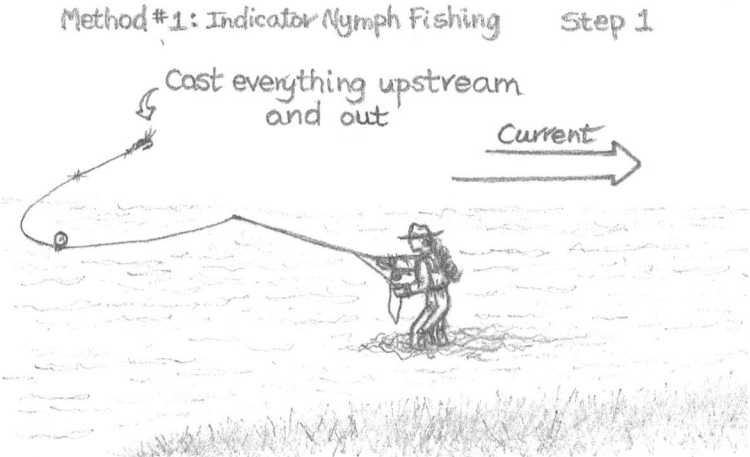

And that's it—Standard Indicator Nymph Fishing. But now I'll add the option of the trailer-nymph rig. How you fish a trailer rig and set the indicator are the same as for Standard Indicator Nymph Fishing. But now, you're fishing *two* nymphs.

In this two-fly rig, the top nymph-fly, the one tied directly to the main tippet, is generally big and heavy (such as a Pat's Rubber Legs or a Burk's Bottom Roller, or at least a Bead Head Pheasant Tail of size 10). The big top nymph is tied to the tippet with a standard fly knot such as the improved clinch (or my clinch), rather than with a loop knot. (I use a standard knot instead of a loop knot for the top nymph-fly because I feel it helps avoid tangles.)

To the hook-bend of this big nymph is tied around one foot (or a bit more) of tippet a size lighter than the main tippet (for example: 3X for the main tippet and 4X for the trailer tippet) so that if the lower nymph-fly snags for good, odds are that the big top nymph comes back: loss minimized. A nymph-fly running medium to small, an imitation or an attractor (could be a Copper John or a Gold Ribbed Hare's Ear or the like, around size 18 to 10) is tied to the end of the trailer tippet with a loop knot. The idea is that the big heavy top nymph will haul down the smaller nymph that can carry only a fraction of top nymph's weight and sink on its own at a fraction of the top nymph's speed.

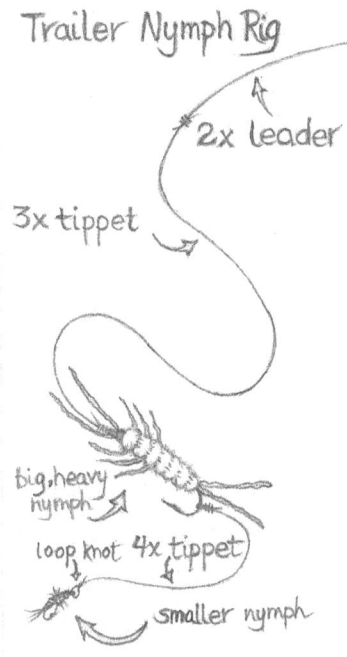

The big-nymph-pulling-down-the-little-nymph mat-ter aside, the trailer rig offers another advantage: a trout gets to choose between *two* different nymphs. And you get to test two nymph patterns to see which goes over best. Your odds of a hookup while fishing two nymphs probably don't double over fishing just one, but they likely go up.

There are lots of trailer-rig variations: small nymph on top and big nymph as the trailer, *two* big nymphs, *three* nymphs (a trailer following a trailer)... Still, the standard big-nymph-on-top/little-nymph-as-trailer remains the most common and most proven arrangement.

Another option is to go with a "dropper nymph rig," which is really a Czech Nymphing rig (it's the Czech rig at least from the top dropper tippet down to the point fly) like the one I offer in "Method #4., Czech Nymphing" to come, and when fished with an indicator must be cast very smoothly with persistent concentration, unless you're curious as to just how intricately tangled nymphs and tippets can get.

Flies for Standard Indicator Nymph Fishing (in order of how frequently I use them for this method):

Bead Head Pheasant Tail; Copper John; Bead Head Prince; Burk's Bottom Roller, Hare's Ear Special; Gold Ribbed Hare's Ear; Pat's Brown Rubber Legs; Bitch Creek; Bead Head Fox's Poopah, Olive; San Juan Worm, Brown; Glo-Bug, Pink; Zebra Midge

(Or, put more economically: with the exception of the March Brown Spider, all the other 11 nymphs.)

Method #2. Hopper Dropper

Hopper Dropper fishing is really a variation of Standard Indicator Nymph Fishing. The first and most obvious way these approaches differ is in the rigs: one uses a conventional strike indicator and the other replaces that indicator with a big, buoyant dry fly, such as an imitation grasshopper. The nymph (or nymphs) hangs from either indicator or floating fly on a length of tippet (and with the indicator, perhaps by some leader too). Fly fishers call the nymph (or any added fly, one that's not the main fly but is worked into the rig along with the main fly) a "dropper fly" or just "dropper." So we have a dropper and a grasshopper imitation: Hopper Dropper.

By both these methods, when a trout takes the nymph, something, an indicator or a dry fly, tells. The angler gets the message and sets the hook.

A less apparent difference between the two approaches is that adjusting the distance between strike indicator and nymph is fairly easy to very easy; adjusting the distance between hopper fly—or just big, buoyant dry fly—and nymph is a fuss. To shorten the tippet between dry and nymph you must cut off the fly and tie it back on. *Lengthening* the dropper tippet is worse.

The Hopper Dropper rig may be slow to adjust, and fly fishers may consequently adjust it seldom or not at all, but it's not really a setup for scraping a stream bed (at least I don't see it that way). It's for those days when the trout will come up to meet a nymph drifting overhead. That's not such a stretch—after all, trout *do* come clear up to take dry flies. (Though there certainly are days when scraping the bottom is the best or only way to hook trout.)

Hopper Dropper fishing also offers trout two very different flies from which to choose: a nymph and a dry. Some days all or nearly all the trout take the nymph. Some days more take the dry than take the nymph. And there are days when the dry and nymph each provide about half the action. Why would some trout ignore the nymph for the dry and others the reverse? Because trout, fish in general, really are individuals. If you find that difficult to believe now, keep fishing. You'll see.

There's a limit to the weight of the trailer nymph-fly. Although an average-size strike indicator can hold up a couple of heavy flies and split shot—and can pop back up after it's dragged under—even a big dry fly can support only so much heft, and, once it goes down, it's probably down for good. Usually the dropper nymph is small but heavy for its size: a real seeker of the stream bed, but not all that heavy on the whole. A bigger, lighter-weight dropper nymph is always an option. I rarely go smaller than size 18 for the nymph, and a heavy nymph of size 12 seems about as much as I'd ask the big dry to support.

In quick currents you want a nymph with enough weight to carry it down and keep it down, so a small bead-head nymph such as a Bead Head Prince or a Bead Head Pheasant Tail is ideal. The standard, only lightly weighted, Gold Ribbed Hare's Ear will do the job if the current is lazy. Something as heavy as the Burk's Bottom Roller? Well, that supporting dry fly had better be truly *big* and *really* buoyant and the Bottom Roller had better be small... On the whole, such a heavy nymph is pushing the limits of the Hopper Dropper setup.

I like the tippet for the trailer nymph in my Hopper Dropper rigs to run one size lighter than the main tippet. After years of snags and big trout breaking me off, I've developed a fondness for losing only one fly over losing two.

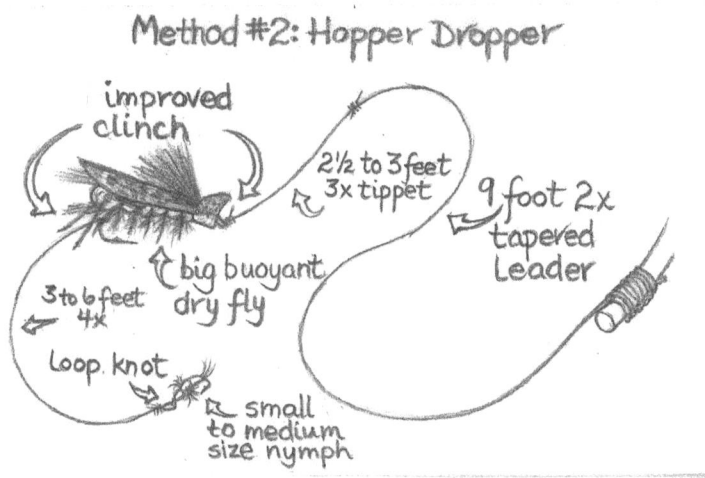

A standard 9-foot tapered leader is my usual choice for middling-size to big rivers and Hopper Dropper fishing. I normally go with 2X for that leader, and add two and a half to three feet of standard 3X tippet to that big dry fly. To the bend of the dry's hook I tie 4X tippet for the trailer nymph. The length of the tippet for the trailer nymph can run quite a range, usually around three to, at the extreme, six feet. Three or four feet is probably typical in my fishing. I tie the trailer-fly tippet to the big dry's hook-bend with a standard knot (such as the improved clinch or Skip's clinch) and the dropper nymph to the other end of that tippet with a loop knot.

(Note, as with Standard Indicator Nymph Fishing, if you see anything suspicious going on with your big dry fly—set the hook immediately.)

Flies for Hopper Dropper fishing (in order of how frequently I use them for this method):

Copper John; Bead Head Pheasant Tail; Gold Ribbed Hare's Ear; Bead Head Fox's Poopah, Olive; Bead Head Prince; Glo-Bug, Pink; San Juan Worm, Brown; Burk's Bottom Roller, Hare's Ear Special (maybe...)

Method #3. Dry and Dropper

"Dry and Dropper" is to some fly fishers just an alternate term for Hopper Dropper fishing. Not to me: when I say "Dry and Dropper" I specifically mean a rig with a *small* to *tiny* and *lightweight* nymph hanging off a dry fly no larger than *modest size*. *Hopper* Dropper fishing, described above, involves a *heavy* dropper nymph and a *big* and especially buoyant dry fly. So I see Dry and Dropper as a cousin of Hopper Dropper, but not at all as an identical twin.

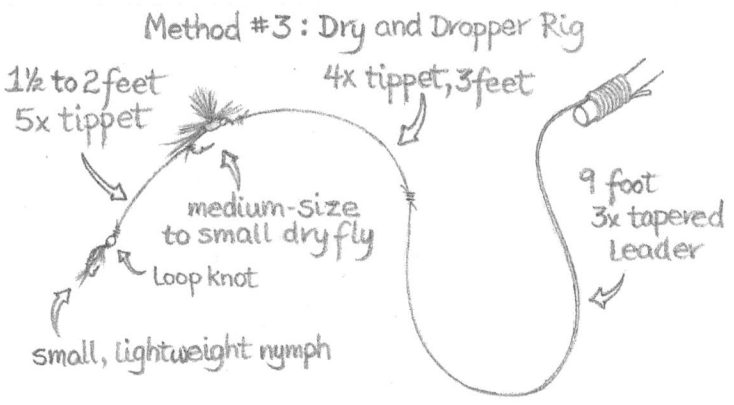

For Dry and Dropper fishing I'm likely to go with a buoyant dry of around size 14, perhaps an Elk Hair Caddis or a Parachute Adams heavily dressed (though I've gone as small as size 18). To the bend of that dry fly's hook I'll tie a foot and a half to two feet of tippet a size lighter than the main tippet (5X for the dropper, for example, if the main tippet is 4X). To the end of that tippet I'll tie on something, as I said, lightweight, perhaps a Zebra Midge in size 18 or 20 (a beadfly, yes, but a bead that tiny won't bother a size 14 dry) or a Gold Ribbed Hare's Ear in size 18, 16 at most (no bead in that one, of course). If I go to a size 14 lightweight nymph, I simply hang it from a largish dry fly, a size 10, or at least a buoyant 12.

I'll tie the tippet to the bend of the dry's hook with an improved clinch (or more likely my own Skip's clinch). I'll tie the nymph to the other end of the tippet with a loop knot.

Look at that foot and a half of tippet for the Dry and Dropper's dropper nymph—right there you leave the Hopper Dropper rig behind. A Hopper Dropper rig typically uses a dropper tippet considerably longer than a measly foot and a half, long enough to let the nymph go at least fairly deep and fairly close to the riverbed.

Leader? A predictable 9-footer with a point of 3X. Tippet? Around three feet of 4X. If the trout are shy I might go finer on leader and tippet (and on the dropper tippet), and longer. For really small streams, I'll go shorter than recommended above on leader and tippet both. Whatever...you adjust for conditions.

Its relatively short dropper tippet makes the Dry and Dropper rig a natural for hatches and what I've come to call "near-rising" trout. And *near*-rising isn't rising: that's an important point. You can read all about near-rising trout earlier in this book in the section on the March Brown Spider. For now, I'll just say, No exposed trout noses, no post-rise bubbles=poor (if any) action with a dry fly.

Those trout, holding high in the swirling current, picking off nymphs or pupae nearing the surface of the water, need a nymph (or something like a nymph), and they need it presented at about their level: they need the Dry and Dropper. (Or perhaps they need the March Brown Spider, a soft-hackled fly, fished on The Swing or on the Upstream Soft-Hackled Fly method, or the Fox's Poopah, a caddis-pupa fly, on The Swing. Just depends on the hatch and the attitude of the trout. You have to experiment until one fly and method or the another works. Anyway, back to the Dry and Dropper.) A trout sees your little nymph drifting up, below what seems another harmless floating insect (your, in fact, not-harmless dry fly), under the mirrored underside of the stream's shifting skin. A moment later you see your indicator dry fly go down, you raise your rod-tip, and you feel the panicked spasms and then angry bolt of a good trout.

The typical catalyst for trout to near-rise is a hatch: mayflies, caddisflies, midges—whatever swims or wriggles up to hatch out atop the river. (Stoneflies creep, of course, so they don't count here.) The trout, at least the bulk of them, happen to select as their target neither the emergers struggling through the water's surface nor the winged adults standing atop it but instead focus on the rising pupae or nymphs. Next, the trout start *near*-rising at the water's surface, showing dorsal fins and perhaps, occasionally, a tail. Possibly some of these trout are taking the adult winged insects off the surface—despite their tendency to act as a group, trout really are individuals and will break with the crowd. Seems about time to toss a Dry Fly and Dropper rig out there.

Flies for Dry Fly and Dropper Fishing (in order of how frequently I use them for this method):

Gold Ribbed Hare's Ear; Zebra Midge; San Juan Worm, Brown (maybe...)

Method #4. Czech Nymphing

There are a bunch of books around now, from fairly new to brand new, that are largely or entirely about this relatively recent approach to nymph fishing in trout streams, an approach that's not so different from the way I first fished a nymph as a kid. I thought, I've got to get this nymph down to the trout, so I'd better drop it in upstream to give it time to sink. I flipped the nymph upstream on little or no line, followed its drift downstream with my rod and, there I was: *almost* Czech Nymphing. The main factor I missed was the leading of the nymph with my rod-tip. (If you don't understand that point, fear not: we'll get to that, very soon.)

Actually, there's more to Czech Nymphing than just that clueless kid (me) dipping a nymph in a creek. There's a component called a "sighter," there are the especially heavy nymphs themselves, and there's rigging.

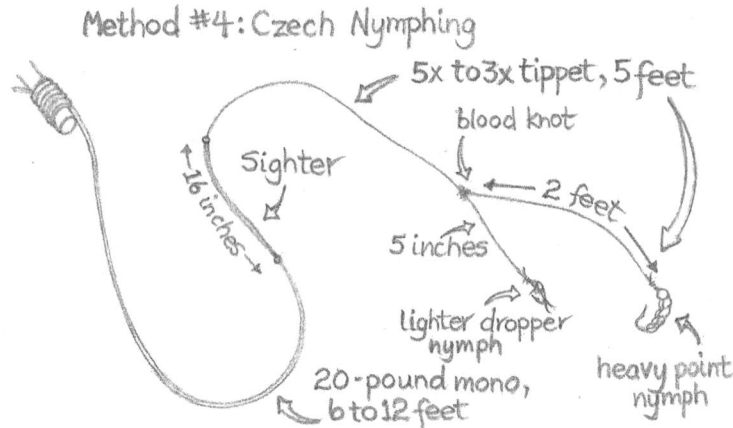

It would be difficult to explain Czech Nymphing without first explaining the style of rig that goes with it. So, here's the rig George Daniel, in his book *Dynamic Nymphing*, offers as "a standard tight-line leader." (George calls all methods related to Czech Nymphing "tight-line" fishing.) On the tip of about five feet of 5X to 3X tippet is tied a heavy point fly. Two feet up the tippet is four to five inches of tippet extending off to the side and tied to a dropper nymph (this dropper tippet is really just a long tag-end from cutting the main tippet and tying the two sections together with a blood knot). Above the dropper tippet is of course more tippet, the remainder of the five-foot section we started with. Next comes 16 inches of heavy, bright-colored monofilament (called a "sighter") of 8- to 10-pound tippet in gold or such. Above the sighter is 6 to 12 feet of some really heavy (20-pound) mono—essentially, the leader. (George includes a little metal hoop called a "tippet ring" at the lower end of the sighter, which you're welcome to investigate, but it's not critical so I skipped it here.) I sometimes omit the sighter and just watch my leader for standard close-in fly-right-under-rod-tip Czech Nymphing (as opposed to long-distance Czech Nymphing, in which the nymphs are tossed out a ways and a sighter becomes invaluable).

Note: no strike indicator. (Unless you want to make the stretch of calling a sighter a strike indicator, which, really, it isn't. I guess...)

What George describes is roughly what I use most of the time for Czech Nymphing, except that I would more likely work with a conventional tapered leader at the top of the system. But then, George knows this tight-line stuff far better than I do and does far more of it than I do.

Some add a third nymph on another four- to five-inch dropper tippet around 20 inches up from the first dropper. That's putting that third nymph pretty far up from the stream bed to compete with those two other nymphs down closer to where the trout hold—and it adds one more bouncing airborne nymph to cast, raising the potential for tangles. That's why I rarely go with three nymphs in my Czech Nymphing rigs and sometimes with only one. That's just my view. A lot of devoted Czech nymphers do go with three-nymph rigs consistently.

How do you choose where each nymph goes in the rig? Well, from what I've read, Czech Nymphing doesn't—or doesn't, depending on whom I'm reading—involve what some call an "anchor nymph," an especially heavy one that sinks ahead of the others, pulls them down and keeps them down. Regardless: I do rig for Czech Nymphing with the heaviest fly on the point. Maybe it's just a habit left over from my indicator fishing years (and as I hope I've made clear, those years definitely continue); but I do like the idea of the heavy point fly going deep and the lighter dropper nymph (or "nymphs") above it trailing in the higher, slightly quicker currents. I've watched such rigs in clear currents under just the right light, and the smaller, higher, lighter nymph looks as though it's swimming against the current—so convincing!

Okay, time to actually do some Czech Nymphing.

1. Starting with the rig all trailing downstream, half cast/half lob the whole thing upstream.

2. Let the rig drift and sink, and once you figure the point nymph is down there fairly close to the stream bed, raise your rod-tip to establish light tension on the flies.

3. Now, *lead* the drifting nymphs with your rod-tip, just a little, to maintain *light* tension so that the sighter will stall or twitch at a take of one of your nymphs; if it does either—set the hook immediately.

4. Continue leading the nymphs to the end of their drift. Then let them swing up at the end—sometimes this is when the strike comes. But the strike can come at any point once the nymphs are in the water. Lob the nymphs upstream again; try to work all the promising water progressively.

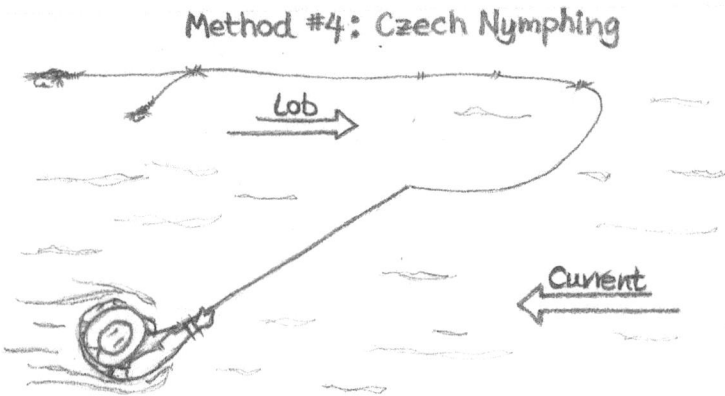

Method #4: Czech Nymphing

Step 1. Wade quietly up to the water you'll fish. Lob the rig upstream, rod-tip low.

Method #4: Czech Nymphing

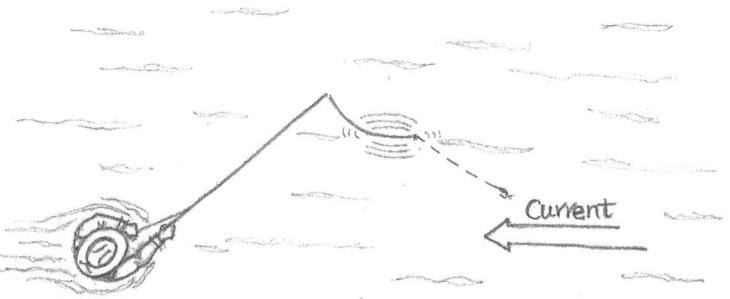

Step 2. Keep your rod-tip low to let the nymphs (or *nymph*) sink.

Method #4: Czech Nymphing

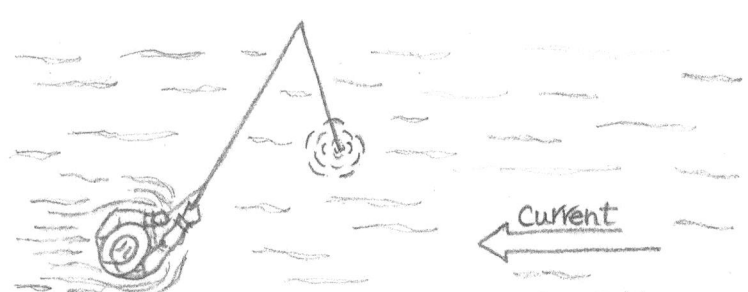

Step 3: Raise the rod-tip to lift the sighter above the water. Swing the rod-tip downstream slightly faster than the drift of the nymphs.

It's standard in Czech Nymphing to set by swinging the rod downstream. Which is a good tactic in Standard Indicator Nymph Fishing too. Fairly often, you'll not see a take of a nymph but *feel* it in the tightening of the line.

Czech Nymphing is normally performed directly below the rod's tip, so you're close to the trout, really *close*. Stealth in both wading up to the fish and in your movements once you're there is wise, or, more accurately, required. But, as I mentioned, you can Czech nymph with the flies out beyond the rod's tip as far as 30 feet (according to the book *Czech Nymph, and Other Related Fly Fishing Methods* by Karel Krivanec, a bona fide Czech).

(Note: don't let all the names for this method confuse you. "Tight-line nymphing," "Euro nymphing," "contact nymphing," and perhaps one or two others I've yet to encounter—they all pretty much mean Czech Nymphing. So, if you're a new fly fisher—welcome to the often confounding language of fly fishing!)

Flies for Czech Nymphing (in order of how frequently I use them for this method):

Burk's Bottom Roller, Hare's Ear Special; Gold Ribbed Hare's Ear; Bead Head Pheasant Tail; Copper John; Bead Head Prince; Bead Head Fox's Poopah, Olive; Pat's Brown Rubber Legs; Bitch Creek; San Juan Worm, Brown; Zebra Midge; Glo-Bug, Pink. (Actually, every fly of the 12 *except* the March Brown Spider, whose standard fishing method is The Swing and is therefore not suited to, or at least not intended for Czech Nymphing. Though a March Brown Spider fished in off-label Czech fashion...maybe?)

Method #5. The Swing

For those whose memories are as porous as mine, I'll say it again: when trout fuss at the top of a stream but leave no bubbles, do not show their noses, that's usually because they didn't quite reach the air—they took something not *off* the water's surface but just *under* it. Failing to notice the bubble and nose, or their absence, is an easy mistake for a fly fisher to make, but it's often a costly one.

Less than two months ago, I tossed dry flies and floating emerger-flies to trout rising in steady abundance, to hook only two or three over the course of an hour and a half. It seemed obvious what the trout wanted: little stonefly adults. They'd taken floating imitations faithfully the previous two evenings. The little stones were fluttering everywhere that shade enveloped the river. One of those refreshingly unambiguous scenarios, right?—little stonefly adults swarming the water, so put on a little-stone dry fly. What's to worry?

I wish now, of course, that I had worried at least a bit, or, better yet, that I'd simply paid attention—enough attention to notice that none of those trout was leaving a bubble. I knew the signs, I should have recognized them. *What* was I thinking?

Clearly, I wasn't thinking, only reacting, my dull mind locked in low gear. But to give myself my due, I *did* come around, if unfortunately late.

Here's what, in hindsight, plainly happened. Despite all those little stoneflies around, above, and surely on the river, the trout were taking something else, something that was more abundant, easier prey, or both—and taking it not at the surface of the water but just under the surface. I never figured out what that something was, and from what I could tell, it didn't matter—those trout took the first fly I swung at them. What clearly did matter is that the fly that hooked those trout was *swung*, and was therefore presented not far underwater, but underwater nevertheless.

So my story ends on a bright (or perhaps only faintly glowing) note of at least some consolation for my once-again injured ego: just before dark I had a sliver of time to swing a fly through the rises —*near*-rises, to be exact—and the result: about twelve swings, nine strikes. So at the bitter end I hooked a few trout in quick succession —thanks to The Swing.

To most fly fishers, The Swing is about fishing soft-hackled flies. (And about fishing flies called "wet flies," which are not represented here because they don't belong in a nymph book.) The first requirement for fishing a soft-hackled fly is the right conditions, which I've already talked about: trout showing at the surface of the water but not leaving bubbles, not exposing noses, that is, near-rising.

But another fine scenario for The Swing is a caddisfly hatch. Many caddis just pop out and fly off right away. The trout get the message: unless you want to keep missing fresh adult caddis, you'd better grab the swimming pupae instead. A fly like the Bead Head Fox's Poopah fished on The Swing is a fine solution. (Although the March Brown Spider can imitate a caddis pupa too...)

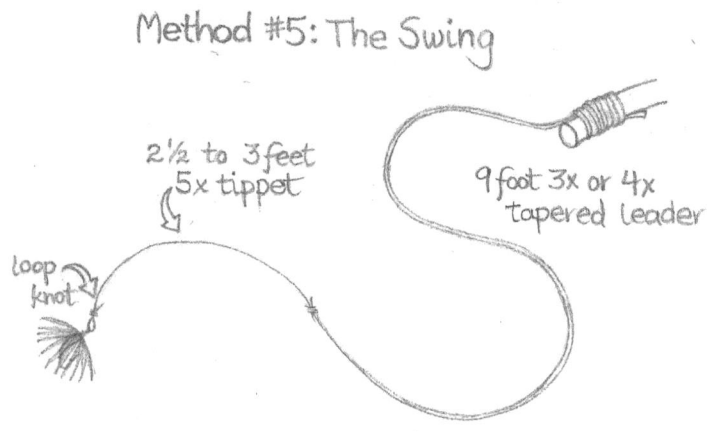

For The Swing, I typically rig up with a full-floating line, a 9-foot tapered leader of 3X or 4X, and about 2 1/2 or three feet of standard 5X tippet. (Fluorocarbon offers two advantages here—it likes to sink, which helps keep an unweighted fly such as the March

Brown Spider submerged, and it's considered harder for trout to see than standard tippet. Cost is not among fluorocarbon's advantages: it's *spendy*.) I tie the fly on with a loop knot, so it can jiggle and sway all it wants. Of course you can and likely should go lighter on leader and tippet if your fish are ultra picky, the water is very clear, the current is slow, or any combination of these. Go heavier if the trout are big and you think they'll overlook the slightly more visible tippet.

So, we're finally to the point of making the actual swing.

1. Cast angling slightly downstream if the current's mild, angling pretty sharply downstream if the current is quick (the steeper angle of the line will slow the swinging of the fly across the current).

2. Hold your rod-tip down and let the fly and line simply drift across the flow; mend the line now and then, usually upstream, as needed, to keep the fly out with the trout as long as possible. So, really, you're letting the soft-hackled fly (or nymph) just trail in the current, imparting no action to it, mending line to keep it from sweeping across the current too quickly.

3. When the fly is straight downstream let it hang there for a few seconds in case a trout followed it in and needs a moment to decide. Then pick it all up and cast it out again. Work your way downstream, so that you systematically cover all the promising water.

Method #5: The Swing

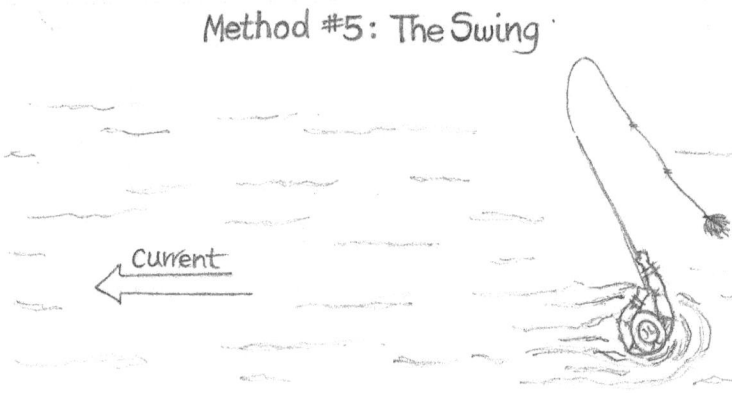

Step 1. Cast the fly across and slightly to steeply downstream.

Method #5: The Swing

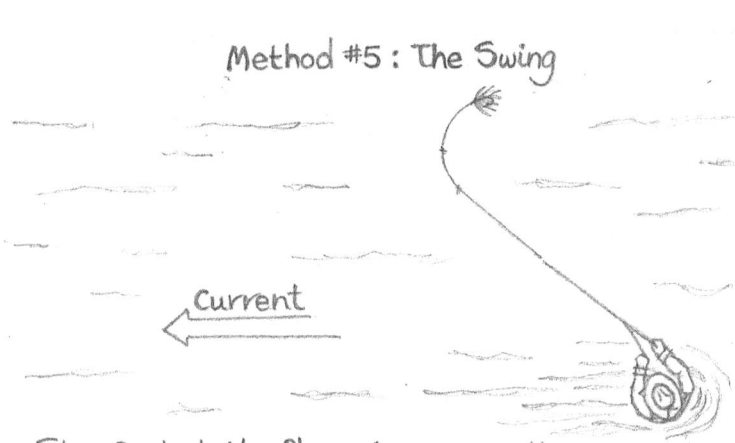

Step 2. Let the fly swing across the current.

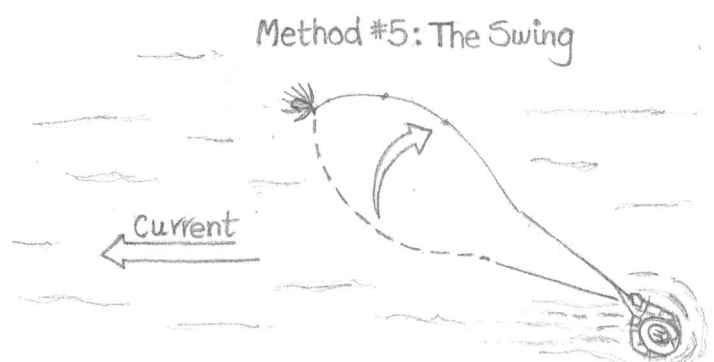

Method #5: The Swing

Current

Step 3. Mend line as needed to slow the swing. Let the fly hang, straight downstream, briefly at the end. Then cast it out again.

You may not see the strike, but you'll feel it, a tug or just a new resistance on the line. When that happens, *don't* set the hook; instead, hold the rod still and hold lightly onto the line—the trout will feel the hook's point, charge off, and come up against the tight line. If in this way you let the trout do the work of hooking *himself* on The Swing you'll land more fish than if you try to sink the hook in.

Wet fly/soft-hackle authority Davy Wotton uses a different approach for setting the hook on a swung fly. He casts, and then holds his rod-tip up fairly high so that much of the line hangs in a broad curve or "belly" above the water; this offers little resistance when the trout does its underwater inhale of the fly. When the tip of the fly line gives the suspicious twitch or other movement created by that inhale, Davy tightens *lightly* on the fish, then holds rod and line frozen. The trout feels the point of the hook, dives for deep safety, and hooks himself solidly. Try it, it works.

If you feel the fly is going too deep (usually because either the fly's too heavy for the speed of the current or the current is just too slow to hold *any* sunken fly up, or, of course, both) or the fly is swinging too slowly, you can retrieve it *a little*, taking in line only in unhurried draws (perhaps with a little rod-tip jiggling). Or you can use the Crosfield Draw—both are described under the Bead Head Fox's Poopah, Olive, which is nymph #9.

Flies for The Swing (in order of how frequently I use them for this method):

March Brown Spider; Fox's Poopah, Olive. (I've seen such standard nymphs as the Gold Ribbed Hare's Ear and Bead Head Pheasant Tail produce on The Swing, so keep an open mind.)

Method #6. Upstream Soft-Hackled Fly

This is an approach I got from Davy Wotton. We chatted through the details over the phone, and then I got his DVD "Wet Fly Ways" and made a study of it.

Davy feels that the long, supple hackle fibers of a true soft-hackled fly, such as the March Brown Spider, get plastered back along the fly's body during The Swing. He sees that as a sort of wasted potential. I've long wondered about it. At one point I'd come to the conclusion that the stiffer hackles of wet flies suit quick currents and the hackles of soft-hackled flies should be limited to light currents. That's reasonable, but partridge, hen saddle: these are feathers of *very* supple fibers. Perhaps too supple to give their best on The Swing regardless of how light the current.

Davy's Upstream Soft-Hackled Fly method lets the March Brown Spider, and other soft-hackles, work its hackle fibers in the most subtle, and I believe most effective way. The fly is drawn just a little, unevenly, and those fibers flex in response. It's almost unfair to the trout. Other than the minor exception of this slight, inconsistent draw, his upstream soft-hackle presentation is almost standard dead-drift dry-fly fishing—with one *major* exception: rather than *seeing* the take of your fly, as you would with a dry fly, you see a secondary indication, such as a twitch of fly line or leader or a fuss where your fly should be. You simply cannot see the soft-hackled fly itself.

Rigging for fishing the Upstream Soft-Hackled Fly? You've guessed already, right? Well, just in case you haven't: it's exactly the same as described in the previous topic, The Swing.

Here's how this goes.

1. Cast upstream and out.

2. Raise your rod-tip to angle the rod mildly up, which creates a hanging belly in the line. As the fly drifts downstream ever closer to you, raise the rod-tip to keep in *very* light contact with the fly—that contact is critical to your detecting a take of your fly.

3. As the fly passes you, lower the rod-tip to keep from dragging on the fly—but you continue to maintain that delicate contact. Point your rod at the drifting fly throughout all the steps.

Method #6: Upstream Soft-Hackled Fly

Step 1. Cast upstream and across. Angle your rod upwards after the line drops.

Step 2. As the line and fly drift nearer, gradually raise your rod-tip higher.

Step 3. As the line and fly move downstream, slowly lower your rod-tip.

Through all this, the soft-hackle remains not far from the surface of the water, and almost drifts free in the current, but gets pulled a little here and there by your efforts to keep only the finest tension on the fly—those little pulls help animate the long, supple hackle fibers (though the whims of the current are already doing the same). When the tip of your fly line darts or twitches or just stalls, you do exactly what you do when that happens with Davy's version of The Swing (method #5. above): you tighten on the fish just slightly, freeze the rod in position and hold the line firmly, and let the trout dive to set the hook on its own.

I've been fishing soft-hackles this new way (a way new to me anyhow) a lot lately on my local streams. It works great: I've landed enough trout by it to confirm that.

The rig? That's easy: it's exactly the same one described and illustrated above for "Method #5. The Swing."

Flies for the Upstream Soft-Hackled Fly (method):

March Brown Spider

18

JUST THE ESSENTIAL STUFF, MADE PLAIN

All the information I've given you up to now is, as best I could make it, clearly explained and neatly organized. But it really is a small mountain of facts and details. They're facts and details you need to know, but it's all just...so much, so much to retain and to keep straight. More than anything else I want this book to be practical—that is, I want it to tell you what you need to know in order to select a promising nymph and an effective method of fishing it so you'll catch trout, regardless of the fishing conditions. What soon follows, then, is everything pared down to the essentials, the essentials organized in a way you can easily and quickly grasp.

Remember, early on, when I asked you to imagine yourself, right now, standing in a trout stream, and then I asked you which fly you should tie onto your tippet? Well, using the information below, you can answer with something like this: "Okay, I've got a hatch of mayflies matching a size 16 hook, trout are sort of rising but leaving no bubbles and they're not showing their noses...—based on Skip's Just the Essential Stuff, Made Plain section, this is Situation #3. So I'll tie on a size 16 March Brown Spider and fish it on The Swing. If that fails I'll try fishing the Spider by the

Upstream Soft-Hackled Fly method. Then, if that doesn't work either, I see that my 'second fly choice' is a size 16 Bead Head Fox's Poopah—but that's not right because that fly imitates a caddis pupa and this is a mayfly hatch. So, I'll try my third 'Fishing method' option: a size 16 Gold Ribbed Hare's Ear with the Dry and Dropper method." And so on.

Nice to have your options laid out simply and clearly, isn't it?

But is the information below as straightforward as it could possibly be? The simple answer: No. I mean, sure, I could present that information like rows of math formulas. So that, instead of saying, "Four times four always equals 16" I'd say, "Under these conditions, fish this specific nymph in exactly this size in this way —*and you'll always catch trout*." I *could* say that, but I could also say, "Exactly two years from this moment it'll be raining lightly in an eight-mile-per-hour breeze in Topeka, Kansas." And I might be right on both the fishing and Topeka's weather, but the point is, I might be dead wrong. Fishing actually is sort of like the weather: no one can really predict it all that well. So the system below is flexible, somewhat loose—*exactly* as it should be—but it really is valid and really will boost your odds of selecting an effective nymph and fishing it in a trout stream in an effective way.

So you have to let the system suggest possibilities, while not adhering to it rigidly. Yes, often you'll be able to just follow the logic below, by letting it guide you to an effective nymph and a method for fishing it, and then catch trout. But nothing's ever certain in fishing. And thank God for that! We'd all soon grow weary of the persistent lack of surprise and suspense and give up fly fishing. But there's no danger of that happening. Fly fishing will always carry plenty of blessed suspense and surprises.

The reason fly fishing is never boringly predictable: trout are sometimes as crazy as people. Even if you know nothing of trout yet, you are a person and therefore know people, which means you know they sometimes behave in ways odd or illogical or both.

Sounds like trout.

So when my proven, normally reliable recommendations below fail, try something else, perhaps something mildly unorthodox. For example, when no trout are showing at the top of the water and what's hatching are mayflies matching the color and size of a size 12 Gold Ribbed Hare's Ear, yet the Hare's Ear isn't getting action, go to a darker Bead Head Pheasant Tail just to see if the change of color stir things up. It might.

If that doesn't do it, try something bolder. Maybe a size *18* Gold Ribbed Hare's Ear. Then, if *that* doesn't do it, try a Bead Head Pheasant Tail in 18. (There's another valuable bit of strategy to remember: when trout refuse a fly, any fly, going down in size can sometimes convince them.)

Still no action? Then it's time for crazy. And, honest: crazy can work. Crazy like drifting a Glo-Bug, under a strike indicator, down through those rising mayfly nymphs. Yes, a Glo-Bug—an *egg*. Another example of crazy: fishing a Zebra Midge when giant stoneflies are just starting to climb out of the water and a Pat's Rubber Legs or Bitch Creek ought to be perfect. Might kill. Again: fishing isn't math, things don't always add up. So if my system to come fails, do not hesitate to try something as odd or even as crazy as what I just described. And then don't be too surprised if that works.

Still, it remains that the recommendations below are sound, proven, and, much more often than not, going to get you into trout.

THE SYSTEM

Situation #1. No Trout Rising (or near-rising), No Insects Hatching

The lack of trout showing at the surface suggests a deep nymph. The lack of hatching insects suggests the trout are open-minded about what they're eating. Therefore—at least in theory—you have a good shot at hooking those trout on either an imitative nymph or an attractor nymph (if you get your fly down to the trout and fish it well, of course). But trout don't worry much about theories. So the logic is sound, and is usually going to be right, but only usually. You have to experiment with flies and methods until some combination works.

But...that's what fishing is.

It makes sense to begin with a nymph that imitates something the trout are used to eating, so I put the imitative Pheasant Tail first; it imitates all sorts of mayfly and stonefly nymphs. But sometimes attractor flies far outfish logical imitative flies, so I put the Copper John second. You get the idea.

And, despite the illogic of it, when trout should be down stubbornly feeding along the stream bed, they'll at times come up enthusiastically for a soft-hackle almost touching the underside of the water's surface—and that's why that fly and its methods appear below.

First fly choices (in order of promise): Bead Head Pheasant Tail, Copper John, Bead Head Prince, Pat's Brown Rubber Legs, Bitch Creek, Gold Ribbed Hare's Ear

Second fly choices (in order of promise): Burk's Bottom Roller, Hare's

Ear Special; San Juan Worm; Bead Head Fox's Poopah, Olive; Zebra Midge; Glo-Bug, Pink; March Brown Spider

Fishing methods (in order of promise):

#1. Standard Indicator Nymph Fishing (for all the flies except the March Brown Spider)

#4. Czech Nymphing (for all the flies)

#2. Hopper Dropper (for the Bead Head Pheasant Tail; Copper John; Bead Head Prince [if tied smallish]; Gold Ribbed Hare's Ear; San Juan Worm; Bead Head Fox's Poopah, Olive; Glo-Bug, Pink)

#5. The Swing (for the March Brown Soft Hackle; Bead Head Fox's Poopah, Olive; and maybe the Bead Head Pheasant Tail and Gold Ribbed Hare's Ear)

#6. The Upstream Soft-Hackled Fly (for the March Brown Spider)

Situation #2. No Trout Rising (or near-rising), But Insects Are Hatching

In this situation, the trout are probably picking off the nymphs or pupae as they rise, from about a foot and a half below the surface to down near the stream bed. So, 1. catch one of the nymphs or pupae and match its size in your nymph. (If you can't catch a nymph or pupa, catch an adult—the size of insect adults is usually close to the size of their nymph or pupa stages), 2. match specifically the form of the insect (the Gold Ribbed Hare's Ear or Bead Head Pheasant Tail for a mayfly nymph, for example; the Fox's Poopah for a caddis pupa), and 3. match the nymph's or pupa's action (example: mayflies swim up usually at a modest pace or they drift, caddis pupae are typically quick swimmers, midge pupae are weak, slow swimmers).

First fly choices (in order of promise. Though that really depends on what's hatching): Bead Head Pheasant Tail; Gold Ribbed Hare's Ear; Bead Head Fox's Poopah, Olive; Pat's Brown Rubber Legs; Bitch Creek; Zebra Midge

Second fly choices (in order of promise. Note: these are illogical and attractor flies, for those uncommon but not rare occasions when trout would rather take something odd than take the hatching insects): Copper John; Bead Head Prince; San Juan Worm; Glo-Bug, Pink; Burk's Bottom Roller, Hare's Ear Special

Fishing methods (in order of promise):

#1. Standard Indicator Nymph Fishing

#4. Czech Nymphing

#2. Hopper Dropper

Situation #3. Trout Showing at the Surface, Appearing to Rise, But Not Exposing Their Noses or Leaving a Bubble (near-rising)

When I've found trout near-rising, it's always been to some kind of hatching insect. I've seen them do it during mayfly hatches, caddis hatches, midge hatches. So, since the trout are onto some insect, you need to figure out what insect they're on. The best way I've found to do this is to catch up a sample or two of the bug by using an aquarium net (I carry one in the big pocket in the back of my fishing vest). Then select a fly close in size and form and color to the natural. If caddis are hatching, for example, try a Bead Head Fox's Poopah or March Brown Spider and fish it not far below the surface of the water. By what method should you fish that fly? Just read below.

First fly choices (in order of promise): March Brown Spider; Bead Head Fox's Poopah, Olive

Second fly choices (in order of promise): Possibly a Gold Ribbed Hare's Ear or Bead Head Pheasant Tail or Zebra Midge

Fishing methods (in order of promise):

#5. The Swing (for the March Brown Spider, Bead Head Fox's Poopah, and possibly the Bead Head Pheasant Tail and Gold Ribbed Hare's Ear)

#6. The Upstream Soft-Hackled Fly (for the March Brown Spider only)

#3. Dry Fly and Dropper (for the Gold Ribbed Hare's Ear and Zebra Midge only)

Situation #4. Trout Rising *and* Leaving Bubbles *and* Exposing Their Noses

Your logical response to these conditions is to forget nymphs and soft-hackles—this is obviously the time for a dry fly or floating emerger-fly. (Neither of which is covered in this book about *nymphs*, of course. But both are covered in my companion book to this one: *Top 12 Dry Flies, How, When, and Where to Fish Them*. Just in case you're interested...)

Still, even when bugs are hatching and trout are truly rising, it's possible that only a *few* of the trout are taking floating insects and that far more are taking the rising nymphs or pupae—then a nymph or soft-hackled fly makes perfect sense. So if you suspect trout are mostly feeding short of the surface of the water, here are your most likely flies and methods to stir up action. (Though, again, you'll probably be better off fishing floating flies.)

First fly choices *(in order of promise):* March Brown Spider; Bead Head Fox's Poopah, Olive: Zebra Midge

Second fly choices *(in order of promise):* Gold Ribbed Hare's Ear, Bead Head Pheasant Tail

Fishing methods *(in order of promise):*

#5. The Swing (for the March Brown Spider, Bead Head Fox's Poopah, and possibly the Zebra Midge, Bead Head Pheasant Tail, and Gold Ribbed Hare's Ear)

#6. The Upstream Soft-Hackled Fly (for the March Brown Spider only)

#3. Dry Fly and Dropper (for the Gold Ribbed Hare' s Ear and Zebra Midge only)

EPILOGUE

So there they are: your 12 top nymphs for trout streams—a truly deadly collection that will nearly always provide you with a fly trout will take. And there it is: all that other information to help you make the most of these nymphs, such as proven methods for fishing them, the best times and conditions for fishing them, what they imitate and a lot more besides. So get out there to your favorite river, stream, or creek and make these great nymph patterns work for you. Catch trout—have a blast!

ABOUT THE AUTHOR

Skip Morris graduated with a degree in English from Central Washington University, and then went out and wrote nineteen ink-and-paper books (published by Stackpole Books, the Lyons Press, and Frank Amato Publications) and around 350 magazine articles on fly fishing and tying flies. He has spoken and taught clinics all over the US, in Canada, and overseas at fly-fishing expos, fly clubs, and fly shops. He and his wife Carol (and an alternately willful, maniacal, affectionate tortoiseshell cat named Olive Penderghast) live on Washington State's lush and lightly populated Olympic Peninsula, amid all sorts of fishing opportunities.

Visit Skip's web-site:

www.skip-morris-fly-tying.com

(Note: Skip teaches a live online writing class—Becoming a Fly-Fishing Writer—during which he covers sentence structures that emphasize and invigorate key words or ideas, how to create pleasing prose rhythms that enhance meanings, how to choose words that work as a team to create powerful moods or images, and a whole lot more. He'll walk you through the current publishing world. At the end he'll even do some writing with you. And all through your time together he'll answer whatever questions you may have. These classes are conducted through Zoom. Just go to Skip's website to read more about Becoming a Fly-Fishing Writer.

Use the contact form there to ask him about the class or to sign up for it.)

Skip's latest titles

In December of 2019 Stackpole Books released Skip's *365 Fly-Fishing Tips for Trout, Bass, and Panfish*. In June of 2020, Skip himself released a small collection of fly-fishing essays as a Kindle book titled *500 Trout Streams*.

Skip's books

Other Kindle books:

1. *500 Trout Streams* (a collection of fly-fishing essays)
2. *Skip Morris 6 Pack, Fly Fishing, Trout Rivers I* (a collection of magazine articles)
3. *The Truth About Jazz Guitar (from one veteran player's perspective, anyway)*
4. *The Truth About Jazz Guitar II (from one veteran player's perspective, anyway)*
5. *Day 6*
6. *The Case of the Case-Carrying Case Workers*

Ink-and-paper books:

1. *Fly Tying Made Clear and Simple*
2. *The Art of Tying the Nymph*
3. *The Art of Tying the Dry Fly*
4. *The Art of Tying the Bass Fly*
5. *Tying Foam Flies*

6. *Concise Handbook of Fly Tying*
7. *The Custom Graphite Fly Rod*
8. *Morris & Chan on Fly Fishing Trout Lakes* (with Brian Chan)
9. *Fly Fisher's Guide to Western River Hatches*
10. *Morris on Tying Flies*
11. *Trout Flies for Rivers*
12. *Fly Tying Made Clear and Simple II, Advanced Techniques*
13. *The Art of Tying the Bass Fly, Second Edition*
14. *Learn to Tie Flies*
15. *Seasons for Trout* (with Hafele and Hughes)
16. *Tactics for Trout* (with Hafele and Hughes)
17. *Survival Guide for Beginning Fly Anglers*
18. *The Salmonfly, Dream Hatch of the West*
19. *365 Fly-Fishing Tips for Trout, Bass, and Panfish*

Hope you enjoyed reading *Top 12 Nymphs for Trout Streams, 2nd Edition* and that it catches you lots of trout and makes fishing for them fun and fascinating for years to come. Please accept my invitation to review the book on Amazon.

Carol Ann Morris illustration

This painting, the earlier painting of a mayfly nymph, and all the illustrations are the work of Carol Ann Morris (as are all the photographs). Visit her Etsy site to see more of Carol's work.

Etsy store:https://www.etsy.com/shop/CarolAMorrisFlyFish

www.ingramcontent.com/pod-product-compliance
Lightning Source LLC
Chambersburg PA
CBHW050832010526
44110CB00054BA/2655